# Educating Librarians
## in the
## Contemporary University

# Educating Librarians in the Contemporary University

## An Essay on iSchools and Emancipatory Resilience in Library and Information Science

*Joacim Hansson*

Library Juice Press
Sacramento, CA

Copyright 2019 Joacim Hansson

Published by Library Juice Press in 2019

Library Juice Press
PO Box 188784
Sacramento CA 95818

http://libraryjuicepress.com

This book is printed on acid-free paper

Library of Congress Cataloging-in-Publication Data

Names: Hansson, Joacim, 1966- author.
Title: Educating librarians in the contemporary university : an essay on
   iSchools and emancipatory resilience in library and information science
   /Joacim Hansson.
Description: Sacramento, CA : Library Juice Press, 2019 | Includes
   bibliographical references and index.
Identifiers: LCCN 2019006528 | ISBN 9781634000581 (acid-free paper)
Subjects: LCSH: Library education--Social aspects. | Information
   science--Study and teaching (Higher)--Social aspects. | Library
   science--Social aspects. | Information science--Social aspects. | Library
   education--Social aspects--Europe. | Information science--Study and
   teaching (Higher)--Social aspects--Europe. | Library science--Social
   aspects--Europe. | Information science--Social aspects--Europe.
Classification: LCC Z668 .H365 2019 | DDC 020.71/1--dc23
LC record available at https://lccn.loc.gov/2019006528

*For Lotta*

# Table of Contents

**Chapter 1:** Building a Profession, with an Education to Go....1

Building a Profession, Slowly......................................................6

A Science for Librarianship......................................................13

Librarianship and the Problem of *Bildung*..............................17

Librarianship as a Welfare Profession......................................21

The Thing with Neoliberalism..................................................25

On Various Institutions and Ecologies....................................28

**Chapter 2:** On Librarianship and Democracy, Soft and Hard.......................................................................37

A Struggle of Ideals..................................................................38

To Recognize the Other...........................................................44

Example: The Library Act of Sweden......................................53

Legislative Ambiguity..............................................................57

Defining Library Practice from Democratic Conflict...........61

**Chapter 3:** Universities and the Speed of Life.........................71

The Contemporary University: A European Perspective.......72

Example: The Entrepreneurial University..............................78

Social Acceleration..................................................86

Academia, Fast and Slow.........................................92

**CHAPTER 4:** The Open Core of Library and Information Science....................................................103

Library and Information Science—An Epistemological Enigma?..............................................................106

Contemporary Perspectives....................................110

**CHAPTER 5:** The iSchool Movement—An Answer to Which Question?............................................125

The Art of Professing Inclusive Exclusiveness.......................127

iSchools and the Notion of Structural Accretion................137

Example: Horizon 2020—The iField Materialized?............142

iSchools—Who Needs Them?...............................150

**CHAPTER 6:** Education for Librarianship—Moving Forward.....................................................157

Revising Concepts, Revising Discourse.................160

Maintaining a Home in the Humanitites............................168

Ethos Resurrected—Towards an Emancipatory Narrative of Librarianship Education....................................176

**REFERENCES**..............................................................183

**INDEX**........................................................................203

## Chapter 1

### BUILDING A PROFESSION, WITH AN EDUCATION TO GO

The summer of 2018 is like no other: in the USA, the holder of the presidency delivers delusional and sinister social media tirades on daily basis, in Europe the most intense heatwave since at least the early 18th century paralyzes the continent, while far-right movements gain strength from Italy in the south to Sweden in the north. Authoritarian sentiments, nationalism, and denial of scientific knowledge are prevalent. Is this what we signed up for? The so-called information age, as it emerged a few decades ago, held the belief that with free and unlimited access to information, society would evolve into a state of enlightenment never before seen. It didn't. Instead we find ourselves in a maelstrom of disinformation, hate speech, and disbelief in the good of humanity, all augmented by social media corporations. Suddenly, being kind and civilized has in itself become suspicious. In the midst of this, Panos Mourdoukoutas, professor of economics at Long Island University, publishes online a casual little essay on the subject of libraries in *Forbes*. It is titled: "Amazon Should Replace Local Libraries to Save Taxpayers Money."[1] The argument is simple:

---

1. Panos Mourdoukoutas, "Amazon Should Replace Local Libraries to Save Taxpayers Money," *Forbes*, July 21 2018.

libraries once had a role in making books and newspapers available to people, but as "third places" like Starbucks have replaced them by offering spaces for information access over a nice latte, their time is now up. Amazon, on the other hand, has a golden opportunity to meet the community need for information and leisure and thus, being today's main global outlet for books and other media, it should consider opening physical bookstores in "every local community" and thereby enhance "the value of their stock." The article sparked such social media outrage that *Forbes* decided to take it off its site within days—it is now only found in cached formats on other sites. The fact that the subject of libraries could create such a response apparently took *Forbes* by surprise, prompting them to back off. Why did this happen? The answer is as simple as the argument put forward by Mourdoukoutas: libraries do not fit into a capitalist market model. They represent something other than just economic logic. They belong to a worldview that sees citizens as complex, living individuals, not merely consumers; that sees local communities as something thriving, instead of layers of customer segments; and that treats information as an emancipatory tool necessary to foster and develop democratic participation, instead of as something that can merely be bought and sold. Christopher Ingraham concludes in a *Washington Post* commentary on the article and its response that "[a]n awful lot of people use and love their public library"[2]—for all the reasons our good professor refuses to accept.

The idea of replacing local libraries with brick-and-mortar bookstores is not a new one; it has occurred frequently in

---

2. Christopher Ingraham, "An Awful Lot of People Use and Love Their Public library, as an Economics Professor Discovered this Weekend," *Washington Post*, July 23, 2018.

various versions and in most countries for at least thirty years. Reactions are almost always strong. We can regard such statements as provocations or as utterances by ignorant individuals, but to do so would be a disservice to both professor Mourdoukoutas and professional librarians all over the world. There is a pattern here and it impacts both professional librarianship and the way in which we view the educational preparations for the practitioners of this profession. Not only are all types of libraries somewhat anomalous in a society built on competition and economic extremism, but educated librarians hold an ethical foundation for their professional practice which is based on the idea of human universals and the unlimited right of every person to be given access to correct and unbiased information and knowledge. In order to maintain this ethos, the education of librarians needs to prepare students for a reality where their profession is put under constant strain. Library and Information Science needs to acknowledge this situation and this constant threat coming from a system which is devoid of the core values fostered by the library profession itself through such acts as literacy promotion for both children and adults, the organization of knowledge resources, and the curation of scientific data. At the same time, Library and Information Science has to face rapid ideological change within the higher education sector that, on a global scale, promotes values that are today much more in line with those promoted by professor Mourdoukoutas. Education for librarianship thus needs to balance demands of very different kinds.

In this book, I will discuss how to uphold this balance. This will be done with the firm conviction that the main basis for legitimacy that Library and Information Science has is due to its explicit connection to librarianship, with a broad understanding of its various practices. The more librarianship is present within it, the more distinct the discipline gets, and the less we see of it, the more likely it is that other disciplines address similar research questions with at least equal pertinence. Not all would agree with this simplified description, and I too will have reason to question this assumption and further refine it, as it gets even more complicated when put in the context of higher education. The changes and developments in today's universities influence and challenge Library and Information Science in the same way as any other discipline. The international development of the iSchools Organization must be seen in light of this. iSchools are, first and foremost, founded to secure the development of the discipline in a new environment for learning and research. How this is done influences the position of Library and Information Science in relation to the library sector and librarianship as a profession.

Librarianship is a profession which rests on a foundation of emancipatory practice. Public librarianship is at the very heart of local democratic participation, academic librarianship is focused on access to unbiased scientific knowledge, and both are united in a struggle against something that has become acute only during the last couple of years: a rapid decrease in trust of knowledge, facts, and research, paired with the sudden emergence of concepts like "fake news" and "alternative facts" targeting professional journalism and political discourse broadly speaking, bringing the very concept of truth into question. Today's society is a challenging environment that calls on librarians to act in certain ways in order to not only maintain their professional ethics but, more acutely, secure freedom of information and democratic values, which are threatened in a way that we are simply not used to. Consequences of this development are visible in library education. Universities are targets for distrust, which is an unusual situation for most of the researchers working in them. A new "knowledge environment," where systematic research and evidence-based professional practice is no longer taken for granted as desired in the political process, is gaining prominence all over the world. For higher education this is a problem as these current developments might be seen as the results of an ideological choice made to prioritize global economic growth through the adoption of a role as "growth-motor" on regional and national levels.

This complex development calls for continuous analysis, and any attempt to contribute to a discussion of the role of Library and Information Science at the intersection between established practices of librarianship and university constraints will quite easily turn into a normative one. It is important to recognize this and see the value of a normative stance, not least as librarianship in itself is a normative profession—normative in the sense that it relates to criteria of objectivity, but rarely of neutrality. Librarianship has always developed in relation to funding structures, user habits, and collection development in ways which demand an ethos providing a clear sense of mission, making the library institution a key contributor to the slow development of not only "free," but more importantly, correct information. The goal is always local democratic participation based on the enlightenment idea that knowledge, unbiased and in the right proportion, brings both individuals and societies towards improvement—structurally, economically, and morally. Librarians have been loyal to this ideology for centuries; educators in Library and Information Science must be, too.

By the end of this book, I will have suggested a position for library research and education that sees librarianship as the very epicenter of a Library and Information Science that is based on emancipatory premises. Today, critical research is present in several areas of the discipline as well as in library practice, perhaps most prominently in issues concerning information literacy and knowledge organization. Research on public libraries has also contributed to a critical understanding of the provision of information and culture from a sociological perspective, which is at the heart of that specific segment of the profession. Before I reach this point, however, I will discuss librarianship and libraries as emancipatory institutions, the ideas underlying contemporary universities, and the iSchool movement, all in order to find both the motivations for and the consequences of these new organizations on practical, epistemological, and political levels. My aim is not to be polemic, but sometimes it helps to present contrasting positions from which a discussion can then be moderated into the necessary, ever on-going negotiations between practice and education, and between ideology and the daily lives of scholars and librarians. But, let me start by anchoring the discussion with a brief historical perspective to see how, when, and where librarianship and library education formed into its current state. I will then discuss how the profession gradually adapted into an integral part of the modern welfare project.

## *Building a Profession, Slowly*
Librarianship has proven to be quite extraordinary in its ability to adapt to political, economic, and social change and restructuring. If there is one thing that has been consistent during the approximately six millennia that libraries and

librarians have existed, it is that they are a socially reproduced good due to proximity to power. Librarians have always been hired by people of aptitude. Libraries have been built as institutional vehicles to secure and display power. They have been used to promote the "goodness" of men with influence, civility, and a love for knowledge, proving the legitimacy of the power of individuals and the sovereignty of reigns. Although librarians have worked in the service of their employers, they have also influenced matters to the benefit of not only themselves, but others as well. On a number of occasions this has had far-reaching consequences. In Roman antiquity libraries were designed to show both contemporary knowledge and maintain a connection to the literary heritage of Greece. Librarians collected and ordered materials according to language and origin in both private libraries and what is generally referred to as the first public libraries—public, of course, in a very limited sense.[3] They didn't have the same ambition as some earlier libraries to hold "everything," nor did they function as did the earliest libraries known to us, in an primarily archival manner, with accounting records and inventories as the main stock, along with religious and mythical texts. Instead, they corresponded to the ideals of the Roman Republic, where free men could seek knowledge not just on practical issues, but for pleasure and the cultivation of civility as well.

The role of the librarian in antiquity is still rather obscure to us, even though we know quite a number of them by both name and deed. It is not until far later, during the 15th century, that we can confirm a kind of librarian who is reasonably

---

3. Lionel Casson, *Libraries in the Ancient World* (New Haven, CT: Yale University Press, 2001), 61ff.

comparable to the information professionals of today. Perhaps the first "modern" librarian was hired in the spring of 1475 to develop that which was to become the Biblioteca Apostolica of the Holy See. On June 15 of that year, Bartholomaeus Platina was formally inaugurated as the first Head Librarian of the new Vatican Library by Pope Sixtus VI, an occasion that has stayed with us by means of documentation, through the papal bull *Ad Decorem Militantis Ecclesie*.[4] Sixtus, who generally is considered the first renaissance Pope, brought to the Holy See a departure from medieval ideals and promoted the value of combining sacred and humanistic learning.[5] His vehicle to achieve this was the establishment of a library that did not, as had been the case for several hundred years, belong to the Pope personally, but to the papal institution as such. He initiated the construction of a kind of communal library built, not least architectonically, on the ideals of the public libraries located just a few kilometers away, over at the Forum Romanum. Platina was given the assignment as both "custos" and "gubenator" at the new library, meaning that he was responsible for its collection development and classification (custos) and its economic and organizational management (gubernator). His position was such that his professional judgement had authority over non-professional views on how to treat the library—including those of the Pope himself, to whom he answered directly. The result was no less than a library which helped establish a new ideology of knowledge. Roman

---

4. David Mycue, "Founder of the Vatican Library: Nicholas V or Sixtus IV?" *Journal of Library History* 16, no. 1(1981): 126.

5. Carmela Vircillo Francklin, "'Pro communi doctorum virorum comodo': the Vatican Library and Its Service to Scholarship," *Proceedings of the American Philosophical Society* 146, no. 4 (2002): 367.

influence was manifest through the division of the library in two major departments, one Roman and one Greek, with the addition by Platina himself of a third room, where the most valuable spiritual and esoteric objects and texts belonging to the Holy See were gathered. This was the foundation of what today is known as the Secret Archives of the Vatican. There was never anything really secret about them, but access was limited to only a close, trusted circle within the clergy. The need for this department was, paradoxically it might seem, a consequence of the decision to let the library be open to the public. Perhaps the most progressive move Platina made was to create a library that was not only open to the clergy but to anyone in Rome and the Vatican, even foreign passers-by—tourists. The breadths of the collections became so vast that the library was soon arguably the most important in the then-known world. Platina still holds a position as one of the most visionary librarians we have ever known. However, he was not a formally-educated librarian. Instead, he was what at first glance seems like a case of Sixtus holding his enemies close: a political revolutionary and a prolific author. He is well known to food historians for having composed one of the most comprehensive collections of recipes of the 15th century, an invaluable source of insight into the taste of his contemporaries and still possible to get hold of.

As always when contemporary fashion and ideals are challenged, librarianship in general is slow to follow, but in subsequent decades, the idea that a library was a strong token of wealth and power was not only present in the clergy but increasingly also in holders of secular power all over Europe. Empirical research became fashionable through, for example, the collection of naturalia on travels of colonization. A large library with valuable books and collections of species and objects from far away was paramount as a display of influence, not least if the materials were brought in as spoils of war. An influential treatise formulating the ideals of the times is the *Musei sive bibliothecae tam private quam publicae extructio, instructio, cura, usus*, written by Claude Clement and published in Lyon 1635.[6] Consisting of two parts, the second of which is devoted to museums and collections of objects, the treatise defines the very essence of how to build a prestigious library, focusing on appropriate architectural design, the need for expensive bindings, and guidance in terms of what should be acquired for those wanting to display their social and cultural position. The librarian is here defined as a benevolent custodian and encyclopedist, knowledgeable in all research areas held in the library.

Clement's depictions of "mainstream" library ideals were, however, not uncontested.[7] A few years earlier, in 1627, it had been challenged by an example of the popular genre of instructive handbooks. This particular one could be considered as a protest treatise, and it would gain influence long after Clement's efforts were forgotten. In his *Advis pour dresser une bibliothèque*, Gabriel Naudé promotes a completely different ideal for librarianship than that common during

---

6. Claude Clement, *Musei sive Bibliothecae tam privatae quàm publicae Extructio, Instructio, Cura, Usus. Libri IV. Accessit accurata descriptio Regiae Bibliothecae S. Laurentii Escurialis: Insuper Paraenesis allegorica ad maorem literarum. Opus multiplici eruditione sacra simul et humana refertum ; praeceptis moralibus et literariis, architecturae et picturae subiectionibus, inscriptionibus et Emblematis, antiquitatis philogicae monumentis, atque oratoriis schematis utiliter et amoenè tesséllatum* (Lyon, 1635).

7. Mathilde V. Rovelstad, "Two Seventeenth Century Library Handbooks: Two Different Library Theories," *Libraries and Culture* 35, no. 4 (2000): 540-56.

this time.[8] He was just appointed librarian by the equivalent of the Mayor of Paris, to care for and develop his personal library. Naudé was, however, no servant. His treatise stresses a number of things which would come to change librarianship forever. He was of course well aware of the relation between the social agency channeled through libraries of those in positions of political and economic influence. Owners should, however, regardless of social position, abstain from ambitions to govern their libraries. As librarian, Naudé demanded full responsibility and a mandate to execute his profession by a logic that went beyond any narrow power display by its owner. The owner should provide means for the development of the library, but in no way interfere with collection development, organization, or managerial choices made. He denounced the necessity of grand and expensive editions and bindings, while claiming content as the guiding principle, and the library's ability to house contrarian views, along with those in line with its owner or otherwise sanctioned by social conventions. Any edition would do, from small pamphlets to expensive folios—form was simply not a priority. Organization of collections should be based not on a static structure, such as the for centuries prevalent Aristotelian division of *Trivium et Quadrivium*, but upon accessibility. The suggested structure was instead taken from the city's booksellers, who organized their sometimes significant stock with the explicit intention to sell books; to be sold, they needed to be found. Thus, the function of the catalog is to help users find what they need and, in order to gain legitimacy for its owner, the library

---

8. Gabriel Naudé, *Advis pour dresser une bibliothèque: reproduction de l'édition de 1644 précédée de L'Advis, manifeste de la bibliothèque érudite par Claude Jolly, directeur de la bibliothèque de la Sorbonne* (Paris: Klinksieck, 1644/1994).

should be open to the public, in a very real sense. In 1627, all of this was highly controversial—some of it still is.

What Naudé did was not just to formulate a practical guide on how to build, organize, and run a library. Through his advocacy, he formulated librarianship as a distinct profession with which owners should not interfere. Interestingly enough, Naudé, like Platina before him, was not a formally-educated librarian. He was a physician and an intellectual held in high esteem within the so-called *République des Savants* in the French capital, a progressive who devoted much time and effort to denouncing and exposing the Rosicrucians spreading across Europe during the first decades of the 17th century. As a physician, he served for a brief period as personal doctor to the French monarch Louis XIII. A year before his demise in 1653, after developing libraries in Italy and France, among those the still world-renowned Bibliothèque Mazarine, he ended up at the Swedish court as personal librarian to Queen Kristina, famously (if not entirely correctly) portrayed by Greta Garbo in the early 1930s.

*Advis pour dresser une bibliothèque* was not in itself unique. Several instructional texts on library development were published all over Europe, but eventually it became the most influential document by far on librarianship from this period. It presents us with a new kind of librarian who, due to the experiences of Naudé himself, lends characteristics to the profession that we usually attribute to, for instance, physicians and other classical professions, not least the more informal ones such as dignity and self-confidence. The physician rules the clinic, the judge presides in the court, the librarian governs the library. Due to this standing, the esteem in which librarians were being held gradually increased not least during the politically formative period between 1790 and 1830 in Europe. As the ideals of liberal democracy were formulated and successively implemented, the need for a new librarian emerged, based on the ideals of professionalism first formulated by Naudé. It is also during this period that we see not only a renewed interest in knowledge as a progressive agent in society, but also the unprecedented growth of libraries, both in terms of numbers and size. There is a thin line between libraries, archives, and museums here, as some of the biggest libraries house collections which can only be described as multimedial: books, pamphlets, maps, globes, and scientific evidentia of various sorts. Furthermore, the growth of materials that needed to be ordered led soon enough to not only a division between libraries (housing created documents) and museums (housing evidentia), but a need for librarians who were not taught as apprentices or who were autodidacts, as were Platina and Naudé, but who were formally educated in the principles of organizing and managing a library. In the early 1800s, formal education starts to gain prominence. Initiatives for early forms of library education are taken in several European countries and some of them prove to be highly progressive. It is beyond doubt that the ideal of the library as a static book repository is already being put to question and an ideal promoting accessibility is gaining momentum. Enter, the educated librarian.

## *A Science for Librarianship*

Ideals were being formed in the emerging difference between technical knowledge which had been emphasized in apprentice education and among autodidacts, and professionality-based principles, or "science." This is a conflict we have seen throughout the history of librarianship, with science focusing primarily on principles for knowledge organization and library management. Few documents have made this clearer than *Handbuch der Bibliothek-Wissenshaft besonders zum gebrauche für Nicht-Bibliotekthekare, welche ihre Privat-Büchersammlungen selbst einrichten wollen* by the Benedictine monk *cum* Bavarian State Librarian, Martin Schrettinger. The treatise, arguably the first in which the term "Library Science" appears in the title, was initially published in 1810 with several subsequent revised and expanded editions. The final and perhaps most-referred-to one dates from 1834.[9] Schrettinger, who at the time of its writing had abandoned his calling as a monk, was instead devoting his considerable energy to developing the Bayerische Staatsbibliothek as Head Librarian.[10] The sheer size of this library, and the rapid ongoing confiscation of the holdings of monastic libraries all over the province which brought in large amounts of additional materials, made new principles for organization and leadership necessary. Ideals formed in the 18th century could no longer stand the pressure of time. The traditional need for librarians to master, for example, German, French, Latin, Hebrew, English, Spanish, and Italian along with universal history and practical diplomacy was deemed obsolete by Schrettinger and he instead formed the idea of an educational curriculum divided into two main parts: the development and organization of collections, and

---

9. Martin Schrettinger, *Handbuch der Bibliothek-Wissenshaft besonders zum gebrauche für Nicht-Bibliotekthekare, welche ihre Privat-Büchersammlungen selbst einrichten wollen* (Wien, 1834).

10. Michael Buckland,"Information Schools: A Monk, Library Science and the Information Age," in *Bibliothekswissenschaft - quo vadis? Eine Disziplin zweischen Traditionen und Visionen: Programme, Modelle, Forschungsaufgaben / Library Science – quo vadis? A Discipline between Challenges and Opportunities: Programs, Models, Research Assignments* (München: K. G. Saur, 2005), 19-32.

issues concerning leadership and management of the library. In promoting this, Schrettinger contributed to the distinction between the ideal of the library being built around an "encyclopedic librarian," and a library which went beyond the individual librarian and was instead subjected to the same mechanisms as any other organization or social institution. Innovative ideas seldom become immediately accepted, however, even if they correspond well to the current *Zeitgeist*, and although we find educational programs for librarianship initiated in several countries in Europe at this time—in Austria in 1864, in France in 1869, and in the UK in 1877—we also see advocates of practice-oriented, apprenticeship learning models holding their ground.[11]

Leopolde Delisle, who became Head of the Bibliothèque Nationale in 1874 is quoted upon the completion of the *Catalogue général des manuscrits des bibliothèques de France* in 1884, as stating that

> un apprentissage est aussi indispensable pour administrer une bibliothèque que pour conduire une bateau, pour construire une édifice, or pour monter, entretenir et faire marcher sans accidents les différentes pièces d'un mécanisme compliqué.[12]
>
> [an apprenticeship is as essential to administering a library as it is to piloting a boat, constructing a building, or assembling, maintaining, and operating without incident the various parts of a complicated machine.]

---

11. Mircea Regneala, "An Overview of Contemporary Librarianship Education," *Studii de biblioteconomie si stiinta informarii / Library and Information Science Research*, no. 9/2005-10/2006 (2006), 16-22.

12. André Masson and Denis Pallier, *Les bibliothèques* (Paris: Presses Universitaires de France, 1961), 57.

He writes this while admitting that "la bibliographie et la bibliothèconomie sont devenue *des sciences* ou des artes dont la complication augmente d'année en année."[13] [bibliography and librarianship have become *sciences*, or arts, whose complications increase from year to year.] Principles and technique. Apprenticeship and formal education. Practice and science—or, indeed, art. The conflict was real and we still live with it one and a half century later.

It is important to note that as educational programs in librarianship were formalized in Europe, most were still not situated in universities, but were mainly found in national libraries. Even so, leading American librarians had their eyes on this development in Europe and the labelling of Melvil Dewey's university department at Columbia University in 1877 as a School of Library Economy did not come out of nowhere. However, when Dewey developed his ideas about how to create a curriculum which would correspond to the needs of the profession, it is important to see that they relate to a very different library environment than those of his European predecessors. The librarian in Dewey's mind was one who would create an institution in the midst of society, working with community building and cultural dissemination among workers and ordinary citizens. The educational discussions in Europe almost exclusively took place in relation to the needs of growing national libraries or those at universities. With the notable exception of the United Kingdom, public libraries in their modern form were still decades away in most parts of Europe. Interestingly enough, this had the consequence that, although Dewey took much of his inspiration from the ideas of the Enlightenment, he created a library school almost fully dedicated to the kind of technical knowledge

---

13. Masson and Pallier, 57.

advocated by those in Europe who wanted to preserve the informal system of apprenticeship. Schrettinger's divisions of knowledge organization and collection development on the one hand, and library management (library economy) on the other is there, but with a highly practical emphasis. As educational, organizational, and managerial ideals, as well as the ideals for librarianship, developed in the decades to come, not least after that break from everything known that was World War I, a new kind of rationality took seat and created demand for innovative ways of thinking on more or less every social issue imaginable. The old world was gone and a new one had to be built. New bases of knowledge were needed for emerging professions such as librarianship. The Carnegie Foundation took on this challenge by funding what in 1923 would become the authoritative version of the Williamson Report, setting the parameters for library education in the 20th century as well as laying the foundation for what would become the international academic discipline of Library and Information Science. Perhaps the most important thing that came out of the Williamson Report was that library education found its way into the university system, and that study in librarianship, or Library Science, became subjected to the same structure of funding, graduation, and admissions as any other academic discipline. This meant that a new distance between the practice of librarianship and the study of library science was created.

## *Librarianship and the Problem of* Bildung

Schrettinger's call for an educational structure for future librarians is still fundamentally vocational, rather than oriented towards the idea of scientific pursuit as a means for individual growth, life-long learning, and civility. Interestingly enough, Dewey's idea of how a librarian should be and function in society is much more in line with the ideals of the Enlightenment, not in terms of curriculum development, but in terms of the individual character demands of those applying to become students at his school. He required a high degree of civility.

Influential early 19th century German humanist Wilhelm von Humboldt, founder of the Humboldt University in Berlin, promoted educational ideals that were built upon the idea that university studies should encourage a foundation for life and not just for practice, and that a professional exam should be seen as just one learning goal—there are also others, much harder to label as "learning outcomes" in the sense we speak of today.[14] This is in the Germanic language area referred to as *Bildung* (with local variations such as *bildning* in Swedish). There are several interpretations of *Bildung*, but no sufficient single definition. A possible translation into English could be "civility." In essence, it is about being civilized, about incorporating knowledge into your own personality in a way which makes you more empathetic and able to critically analyze the world around you, about constantly seeing the bigger picture. It is a concept which is closely connected with the concept of class and, which is relevant for librarianship, it gained renewed relevance as the working class has been admitted to higher education, step by step during the 20th century.

In the Scandinavian tradition, there are three distinct versions of *Bildung*: a conservative, a liberal, and an emancipatory. Conservative *Bildung* connects to, and is

---

14. Thomas Karlsohn, *Universitetets idé: sexton nyckeltexter* (Göteborg: Daidalos, 2016), 96-105.

achieved by, studies of classical philosophy together with a defined canon of European literature and art. It aims to create social stability, with the notion of cultural continuity at its core; it thus appeals to the upper and ruling classes of any given society. The liberal version of *Bildung* is, in political terms, connected to social-liberalism much along the line of John Stuart Mill: through knowledge of social structures and economic mechanisms, individuals can become both entrepreneurial and compassionate; striving to earn money then never overshadows the social obligation to work for decent living standards, both materially and spiritually, for the masses. It is, however, still a concept for the ruling classes. The emancipatory version of *Bildung* takes much the opposite stance, that workers should acquire knowledge, skills, and manners in a way which creates opportunities for them to take part in economic, social, and political development. Emancipatory *Bildung* is significant because it emanates from the working classes, and not the ruling elites. It is this version of the concept that, subsequently, becomes the bedrock of the Swedish and Scandinavian versions of representative democracy, and perhaps the most fundamental feature of the welfare state that flourished between approximately 1950 and 1990. In the USA and the UK, the liberal version of *Bildung* can be seen in the system of philanthropy that, amongst many other things, led to the expansion of the public library system. It is based on a civilized, social-liberal capitalism, but still maintains rigid class structures through a top-down, giver-receiver relationship between classes, which are firmly kept apart. The consequence is the social reproduction of class and gender structures rather than democratic emancipation, as Alexandra Carruthers has shown.[15] It further illustrates the consistency of the claim that libraries stay close to power. In the Gilded Age, they were in the hands of crude capitalists, and in developed democracies libraries continue to be part of the institutionalization of power. Little by little, public libraries do become owned by the people.

Williamson suggests not only that formal education in librarianship should be placed in universities, but that it should consist of individual studies for at least four years followed by a year at a Library Studies department. This is a major difference from the more technical ideals of Dewey, but what is perhaps even more interesting from a sociological point of view is that he makes a clear distinction between professional librarians and those doing clerical work in the libraries. This distinction is still important. While librarians educated in library science perform their profession work, clerical work could be done by anyone with the equivalent of a high school education and a short introduction to library work. The hierarchy is paramount:

> [w]hatever the method employed for recruiting clerical workers, it is of the greatest importance not to overlook the fact that training is necessary for the best results. Without the trained clerical assistant, the professional worker [librarian] will be overburdened with responsibilities for detail from which he should be free in any properly organized library.[16]

---

15. Alexandra Carruthers, "Social Reproduction in the Early American Public Library: Exploring the Connections between Capital and Gender" in *Class and Librarianship: Essays at the Intersection of Information, Labor and Capital*, eds. Erik Estep and Nathaniel Enright (Sacramento, CA: Library Juice Press, 2016), 25-48.

16. Charles C. Williamson, *The Williamson Reports of 1921 and 1923: Including Training for Library Work (1921) and Training for Library Service*

Beverly Lynch convincingly shows how the subsequent implementation of the Williamson Report helped elevate the American library sector to full professional status.[17] She also points out the interesting fact that educational programs in Library and Information Science sometimes distance themselves too much from the profession in order to meet, for instance, university policy, while others tend to emerge in their place with the blessing of the professional field. This is a kind of self-regulatory process which is important in professional theory as we see here a well-known problem: the need for education to be separated from the vocational, but relevant as a platform for professional conduct and execution. To succeed in maintaining such a balance is a truly delicate and sometimes underestimated matter. However, before I embark a discussion on how this balance is kept today, it could be valuable to provide a brief reminder of what it means to be a profession and how librarianship meets such criteria. I do this not because it is necessary anymore to argue for the professional status of librarians, but simply to show that librarianship is plagued by the same problems as many others: those forming a specific type of professions which are sometimes labelled "welfare professions."

## *Librarianship as a Welfare Profession*

The concept of welfare professions relates in a rather specific way to the development of various versions of the welfare state in Scandinavian countries, and should be seen as related to the perhaps more common, although outdated, concept of

---

*(1923)* (Metuchen, NJ: Scarecrow Press, 1971), 11.

17. Beverly P. Lynch, "Library Education: Its Past, Its Present, Its Future," *Library Trends* 56, no. 4 (2008): 931-53.

semi-professions. The term has, however, a useful sense in that it signifies that there is an ethics or moral direction in the content of the professions, rather than just indicating that we are dealing with "almost real" professions, which has been a reoccurring criticism of "semi-profession" as a concept. Librarianship is a typical welfare profession in that sense, together with, for example, social work, nursing, and teaching.[18] They have all acquired at least most of the formal requirements connected with traditional professions, but with less emphasis on excluding mechanisms. Jan Nolin describes four stages of the formulation of a theory of profession, in which profession is traditionally characterized by a number of basic criteria, such as:

- A formal university-level education
- Professional organizations or associations
- Established publication channels
- Ethical codes or guidelines
- Systematic continuous competence development.[19]

Welfare professions have gradually come to meet these criteria during the 20th century and have developed a more uniform character internationally during the last forty to fifty years. They have all been institutionalized as part of establishing a societal structure that was deemed necessary to create a democratic model built on equality in both social and economic terms. As they have developed in a democratic

---

18. Monica Kjorstad amd Maj-Britt Solem, *Critical Realism for Welfare Professions* (London: Routledge, 2018).

19. Jan Nolin, *In Search of a New Theory of Professions* (Borås: Högskolan i Borås, 2008), 16-26.

structure from the start, they tend to put less emphasis on the excluding character of the basic criteria than do traditional professions.[20]

In Sweden, Norway, and Denmark, the development of professions defined in relation to democratic structures took off in the 1920s, helping to elevate these three extremely poor countries on the European periphery to some of the most socially and economically advanced—and equal—societies in the world. Without a very deliberate and consistent re-institutionalization of political and social structures, and a reconstruction of economic governance, this would not have been possible. Welfare professions should therefore be seen not just as developments of older practices (they all have predecessors), but first and foremost as emancipatory professions that have the very specific task of being tools for the achievement of social and economic justice and equality. They put to work the ideas of free health care, free schools, free higher education, free and equal access to information and culture—things necessary to create a good society. It is a strong mandate. Up to a certain point this mandate made several professions all run in the same directions. Librarians, teachers, and university professors were all part of a process of the democratization of access to knowledge. When Tony Blair ascended to the position of Prime Minister in the UK in 1997, repeating his famous "education, education, education" mantra inspired by the ideas perhaps best formulated in Anthony Gidden's *The Third Way*, he tried to reshape the Scandinavian welfare models to fit the arguably more neoliberal and competitive environment of the postmodern

---

20. Magali Sarfatti Larson, *The Rise of Professionalism: Monopolies of Competence and Sheltered Markets* (New Brunswick, NJ: Transaction Publications, 2013), 104-135.

UK.[21] It didn't work out very well, as several critics pointed out early on.[22]

The problem of "upgrading" social democracy was clearly visible also in the Scandinavian countries, where the welfare state construct suddenly found itself under scrutiny in the early 1990s. The UK experiment sort of bounced back. The reason why it ran into trouble is quite simple. First of all, the Scandinavian welfare state (in any of its versions) was never flawless; no political system or model is. It required a kind of fundamental social *status quo* and was not driven by an idea of development or change and it thus had no real sense of where social development should go once basic social security and economic equality had been, at least theoretically, achieved. This particular flaw created a vulnerability to goal-oriented neoliberalism against which it subsequently proved defenseless. Welfare professions were elevated within the social construct of the welfare state as emancipatory tools. Their roles were defined by the idea of solidarity channeled through a highly progressive tax system that would create sufficient funding for the necessities for democratic development: knowledge, health, reasonable working conditions, and individual value not tied to productivity but to each person for her or his own sake. Basically, the welfare state was built on the Marxist axiom *from each according to his ability, to each according to his needs*. This is the radical idea of sharing; in such a worldview, libraries tend to be important.

---

21. Anthony Giddens, *The Third Way: The Renewal of Social Democracy* (Cambridge, UK: Polity Press, 1998).

22. Anthony Giddens, *The Third Way and Its Critics* (Cambridge, UK: Polity Press, 2000).

## *The Thing with Neoliberalism*

The ever-ongoing international discussion of whether Library and Information Science education teaches the right things and attracts the right students is a given consequence of professionalization and one of the key differences from the pre-professional stage with its more technique-oriented vocational education or apprenticeship. The distance which is created between applied and theoretical knowledge is exactly the difference that shows up between the principles suggested in Schrettinger's *Bibliothek-Wissenschaft* and the Graduate Library School in Chicago, stemming from the ideas put forward in the Williamson Report. The professionalization process took place at different times in different countries. In Sweden it emerged in two stages, first through national educational reform in 1993 which put a halt to education for librarianship and was replaced by Library and Information Science, and then in 1999 with the European Bologna Declaration which led up to the uniform graduation system we have in the European Union today. This is one explanation for why, for instance, the iSchool movement would not have been able to create such a major international expansion as it has today in, let us say, the period before 1989 when the Berlin wall still symbolized a static division of the developed world. The educational standardization required was just not there. What was missing was an ideological hegemony on a global scale.

Shared wealth is not a priority in neoliberalism and when the hegemonic shift came, gradually, during the 1980s and 1990s, the rules for, and roles of, social institutions and professions had to be rewritten. It is in this process that a differentiation between the educational system and librarianship becomes vindicated. Higher education institutions of all sorts adapted with relative ease to new terms for governance based on competitive practices. But librarianship struggled to keep its core emancipatory mission with its potential to question the inequalities built into the neoliberal system—inequalities that are not just a consequence of but a means of achieving this particular social model's unique definition of social progress: *economic growth*. Suddenly, this potential had to be held back. The differing degrees to which the educational sector and the library sector could adapt to the neoliberal agenda started to raise concerns about how to legitimize and organize education for librarianship. A main problem was how to harmonize the two entities in order to move in the same direction, for the benefit of the profession. Perhaps the most common way of doing this has been to create a narrative in which libraries and professional librarianship are parts of the information industry. In creating this narrative, there is also an element, as there must be, of reciprocity in that there has developed a strong undercurrent of research and teaching in Library and Information Science that makes use of emancipatory theory in analyses—and development—of library practice.[23] The role and position of education for librarianship in this competitive environment is both interesting and necessary to analyze, both from an epistemological and an organizational viewpoint.

Although the global ideological takeover by neoliberalism is of a scale perhaps unseen in the history of mankind, it emerges with some variety in different countries. In the USA, its development has been less dramatic than it has in,

---

23. Gerald Benoit, "Critical Theory and the Legitimation of Library and Information Science," *Information Research* 12, no. 4 (2007): paper colis30.

for instance, Sweden and most other European countries. In the USA, competition and unscrupulous capitalism has been inoculated into the DNA of its society since at least the Gilded Age with its Rockefellers and Carnegies. In Sweden on the other hand, using strict and progressive taxation as a tool to maintain a strong public governance over the market was never really controversial. The shift was marked by the break of social democratic hegemony in 1991, as the first conservative government for over seven decades was elected. New Public Management was introduced as the guiding principle of public authorities, hence also in libraries. In 1992, a highly influential anthology, *Biblioteket som serviceföretag* (*The Library as a Service Enterprise*) was published, suggesting a new era of thinking about the mission of libraries, primarily public ones.[24] It advocated a stronger focus on user demands and a shift in vocabulary adapting to a more commercialized environment, suggesting the term "customer" instead of "user," along with an increased priority for information provision rather than cultural participation. Discourse sparked by these suggestions led to several attempts to "privatize" public libraries in counties all over the country, all failing badly. There was simply no commercial incentive in libraries at that point in time and the system was not prepared to support such initiatives. Today, as New Public Management is not so new anymore, business solutions have emerged in Sweden, as in most countries, that were not foreseeable in the early 1990s. This is primarily due to technological developments, but also to the global idea of economic growth as the key to prosperity. Once this trope took root in Europe, the

---

24. Barbro Blomberg and Göran Widebäck, eds., *Biblioteket som serviceföretag: kunden i centrum* (Stockholm: Forskningsrådsnämnden, 1992).

European Union made sure that incentives were created to make actual change happen through research, innovation, and management. By means of various outsourcing practices, libraries of all kinds have been subjected to privatization in a way which has proven viable. For public libraries, this is sometimes a problem as they have an exclusive legitimacy through tax-funding—that is, common ownership. It has also affected the prerequisites for the education of librarians in Library and Information Science departments.

## *On Various Institutions and Ecologies*

In an important article published in 1996, Nancy Van House and Stuart Sutton define Library and Information Science as part of two distinct, but interacting "ecologies"—that of the information industry (library profession) and that of higher education. One central conclusion is that the gap between the knowledge interests of the profession and those of higher education is set to morph into new forms. One problem is that, on the one hand, Library and Information Science research is tightly connected to practice-oriented, tool-constructing, and management-related issues, and on the other, developments create a need to reassess values tied to the non-profit, democratic base of librarianship. They conclude:

> [P]rofessional values may need critical reassessment. Public service and information as a public good are fundamental values of public and not-for-profit libraries. The idea of information as a commodity and the norms and values of the private sector appear to many current LIS professionals to be inherently at odds with the profession's traditional values. Yet much of the innovation in information services and products is taking place in the for-profit sector. Libraries and LIS professionals need to neither abandon these principles nor defend them uncritically. If the information world is to be increasingly rich

with for-profit, fee-based information services and products, as well as free and low cost ones, LIS professionals must ask what role they wish to take in these new technologies, services, products, and institutions.[25]

When this was published, the rapidly-growing information industry was a core challenge for the library profession, with its traditionally secured inertia bolstered through professional organizations, educational structures (in Van House and Sutton's case, the American accreditation system), and a widespread culture of practice which holds a built-in skepticism towards change and innovation as such. Today this situation still exists, even as technology has moved forward significantly and we have reached the end of the information society trope, as data has become the center of interest largely at the expense of "information," and as the idealistic visions of the internet are now part of the ancient history of its existence. Discourse is not least manifested through discussions about—and actual practice in—the development of the iSchool movement and its ability to maintain any ideals other than those related to the for-profit information industry. As this development is now no longer an exclusively American affair, different traditions come into play, shaping and reshaping the idea of Library and Information Science education, trying to meet ever-changing professional demands. The question is, of course, *how much* has actually changed? I will let this question hang for a while as I will later engage in a deeper discussion about the implications of the iSchool movement on the relation between Library and Information Science

---

25. Nancy Van House and Stuart Sutton, "The Panda Syndrome: An Ecology of LIS Education," *Journal of Education for Library and Information Science* 37, no. 2 (1996): 144.

and librarianship. Before we move on to contextualize this relation on a somewhat broader scale, we should pause for a while on an interesting follow-up to the above-quoted article. It was published by Stuart Sutton, alone this time, three years later, in 1999. In his "The Panda Syndrome II: Innovation, Discontinuous Change, and LIS Education,"[26] he asks whether Library and Information Science educational institutions manage to provide the library and information sector with professionals capable of addressing the necessary measures needed in order to advance both librarianship and its relevant educational institutions, in the light of perpetual change. The two "Panda Syndrome" articles are important because of their ability to pertinently formulate some basic problems concerning the relation between the information industry, professional librarianship, and educational needs. This pertinence can be ascribed not only to the brilliance of their authors, but just as much to their timeliness. The second half of the 1990s is not just the foundational period when information and communication technologies that shape our daily lives today first emerge on a broader scale. They are also the years when we see an international harmonization and adaptation of educational systems. In Europe, the 1999 Bologna Declaration had implications for Library and Information Science through the conscious merger of commercial and democratic values by means of technology, much in line with that which is discussed by Van House and Sutton. This suddenly put Library and Information Science at the center of development in a way that few within the field realized, even though there had been sporadic recognition

---

26. Stuart A. Sutton, "The Panda Syndrome II: Innovation, Discontinuous Change, and LIS Education," *Journal of Education for Library and Information Science* 40 no. 4 (1999): 247-62.

of this much earlier, not least within the early 20th century European documentation movement.[27]

Sutton revisits the idea of librarianship as being situated between two "ecologies," both now subject to rapid change. Each of them exhibits a rich history which has developed incrementally, with practices close to each other but still in parallel, and which are central to their perceived legitimacy. In librarianship this may be the combination of teaching practices and collection management through classification and cataloging, dealt with on the basis of professional knowledge of the information behavior of users and the principles of the Anglo-American Cataloguing Rules (AACR2) or the Dewey Decimal Classification System. In some sense, this combination of practices defines the core of the profession. In higher education, corresponding development can be seen in the conflict between practices of new educational formats such as distance learning and flexible learning models, and those of traditional lectures and seminars. In research, there has been an increased tension between epistemological priorities. Basic research focusing on the generation of ideas, and applied research focusing on turning these ideas into the innovation of products for a market have been increasingly put up against each other. The situation for librarianship is said by Sutton to be characterized as one of "punctuated equilibria," where libraries and Library and Information Science education both have to find a way to maintain the advantages of having certain practices

---

27. Ronald E. Day, "Tropes, History and Ethics in Prodessional Discourse and Information Science," *Journal of the American Society for Information Science* 51 no. 5 (2000): 469-75; Alex Wright, *Cataloging the World: Paul Otlet and the Birth of the Information Age* (Oxford, UK: Oxford University Press, 2014).

which have become refined over long periods of time, and still be open to letting go of those parts that have become obsolete through both rapid technological change and new institutional roles and functions made possible through innovation in related, external markets. The change from slow incremental development into fast discontinuous change makes it necessary for both the professional field and its related educational programs to reassess the core of what should be kept and what should be left behind. The question is whether Library and Information Science as a scientific discipline and educational practice can meet the library sector *in an agreement* on which parts to keep and which to leave behind, in order to rewrite the relevance of librarianship.

> [T]here is a perceived break between the context of community practice and academic research since the intractable problems of the professions appear not to induce research resulting in innovative solutions capable of changing the community's standard practices.[28]

As will be shown, this rhetoric hasn't changed much since the late 1990s; it has just taken new forms. The question, however, still lingers. The choice of what to keep and what to get rid of in librarianship and library education is still unresolved. It is obvious that numerous practices that were seen as undisputed core competencies by Naudé and Schrettinger can no longer motivate the same interest in either education or practice. Skills in practical classification and cataloging are required for fewer librarian positions and collection development continues to take on new dimensions through new patterns of publication, not the least in

---

28. Sutton, "The Panda Syndrome II," 258.

scientific communication. In parallel to this, user relations have also evolved. Apparently, what is irrevocably crucial to maintain in librarianship is thus not found in elements of practical technique, but perhaps rather on the level of ideas and principles, and within the fundamental mission of any given library. This implies that we do indeed have a conflict between, on the one hand, the not-for-profit library ideals of democracy, user participation, and (genuinely) free access to knowledge and information, and on the other, the for-profit information industry ultimately driven by that which drives all private enterprise: the generating of revenue for its owners. One demands time, consideration, and incrementalism; the other feeds on discontinuity, innovation, and speed. The gulf between the two has perhaps never been deeper than today. The question is how to deal with it. One somewhat speculative answer is that no punctuated equilibrium is sustainable. Along with their general academic virtues, the Panda Syndrome studies both fail to recognize the problem of lost social narratives and instead choose to address discontinuity as something both given and, ultimately, desirable. This is not an unusual conclusion in Library and Information Science research; on the contrary. It has, however, tended to create uncertainty both within the discipline and within librarianship, often resulting in a nervousness seen in the uncritical advocacy for anything new, whether that be a technological solution or a managerial model, all fueled by a fear of being "left behind." I claim that we live today with the consequences of the moral laziness and lack of critical consciousness in much of 1980s and 1990s Library and Information Science research. Without a substantial narrative it becomes difficult to find a direction and a meaning in either of the two "ecologies," not least within Library and Information Science as a scholarly discipline.

In order to create an understanding of the development of Library and Information Science as a relevant educational platform for the library profession, we need to take this situation seriously, and ask how to develop a democratic narrative for both professional librarianship and Library and Information Science in order for them to develop together as constructive parts of society and in an international political environment that seems to move too quickly for its own good. In meeting the many pressing societal challenges of today, it is important to choose. The information industry is certainly at the heart of the development of what Hungary's current Prime Minister Victor Órban calls the "illiberal" society—a far cry from the nirvana-dreams envisioned in Silicon Valley in the 1990s. Which challenges are the most important for Library and Information Science and which should be prioritized by the library profession? A starting point for such an analysis is to define a broader understanding of the current processual changes in society, such as doubt in universalism and new forms of class structures. A contextual understanding is not just important for describing the relation between incremental and disruptive change, but is instead something which can be used as a trope for bringing together all these pieces, that today seem to be up in the air, into a collective narrative. I will do so with the help of three lines of thought that have emerged within critical theory: rational communicative action, the need for recognition of the other in conflicts, and social acceleration. It is now time to look at what Brenda Dervin, in her now legendary keynote address to the first ISIC conference in 1996, called "an unruly beast"—the social context.²⁹

---

29. Brenda Dervin, "Given a Context by Another Name: Methodological Tools for Taming the Unruly Beast," in I*nformation Seeking in Context: Proceedings of an International Conference on Research in Information Needs, Seeking and Use in Different Contexts, 14-16 August, Tampere, Finland*, eds. Pertti Vakkari, Reijo Savolainen and Brenda Dervin (London: Taylor Graham, 1996), 13-38.

# Chapter 2

## ON LIBRARIANSHIP AND DEMOCRACY, SOFT AND HARD

The Panda Syndrome studies are emblematic of the general sentiment still present in contemporary Library and Information Science. Incremental change in librarianship is problematic as society is characterized by punctuated equilibria, and discontinuous change is an impediment for a critical understanding of the social function of both academic and public librarianship. Trust in the belief that the for-profit information industry has the ability to maintain the same kind of legitimacy for libraries and librarians as their traditionally non-profit versions, in short that corporate priorities equal democratic ones, also goes hand in hand with a general distrust of public institutions today—a distrust that now has proven detrimental for the ability to keep the social fabric together. However, it could be different.

In order to understand Library and Information Science as part of, on the one hand, an ideologically adaptive, increasingly corporate and international higher education system, and on the other, the fundamentally emancipatory function of professional librarianship, we need to find a way to build a narrative within which it is possible to understand 1) the mechanisms transforming higher education into a support structure for global capitalism, 2) the shape Library and Information Science takes in such a transformation, and 3) the struggle for legitimacy in the library sector. It is not enough to conclude that, in a somewhat simplified way of expressing it, both Library and Information Science and the library sector should "sharpen up" and accept a condition of punctuated equilibria and while doing so, uncritically meet a constantly changing reality as part of the commercial information industry. A conclusion like that is paradigmatic. There can be no sustained punctuated equilibria or an ever-ongoing revolution, and no such thing as constant social disruption is possible. At times things need to calm down, and democracy is not made out of speed. On an epistemological level, this is the problem of post-modernism itself. If any of these disruptive happenings or states should occur, and indeed they do from time to time, they must be defined in relation to a problem or a situation against which new ideas or paradigmatic presuppositions can react. In many cases, not least in the information industry, this reaction consists of addressing well-known issues with new technological solutions—old problems, but new tools.

## *A Struggle of Ideals*

The tension between incremental and revolutionary change has been increasing ever since Van House and Sutton formulated their conclusions and, in hindsight, part of their argument seems almost like a premonition. If we want to connect the situation of librarianship and library education to a larger social perspective, it is because it is important to look for the root of the problem. Incremental change is not a problem in itself, nor is any other form of change or development. It becomes so if, suddenly, it is defined as something which is in the way of something else, such as a reconsideration of the social construct itself. Librarianship and education, as well as most other tax-funded institutions and practices, have all been subjected to such reconsideration through the rise of neoliberalism. Neoliberalism is, however, no longer neither new, nor truly liberal. It never really was. Still, it has, with some notable exceptions, been remarkably absent in explanatory models concerning Library and Information Science.

In his book *Dismantling the Public Sphere*, John Buschman describes this movement as an ideological dismantling of the very prerequisites for librarianship, with reference to the social theory of Jürgen Habermas and the gradual but relentless introduction of late capitalist public management ideals and principles into library management and user relations.[1] Libraries, particularly public libraries, have always been part of liberal democracy through the institutional function that they have upheld until the last quarter of the 20th century, with only little variation between countries and regions. In such an environment, stability and striving for consensus is desirable. Stability, endurance, and incremental change processes provide prerequisites for communicative action in Habermas' sense; democratic participation is made possible as the rules for public discussion and behavior are clear and

---

1. John Buschman, *Dismantling the Public Sphere: Situating and Sustaining Librarianship in the Age of the New Public Philosophy* (Westport, CT: Libraries Unlimited, 2003). See also John E. Buschman, "The Social as Fundamental and a Source of the Critical: Jürgen Habermas," in *Critical Theory for Library and Information Science: Exploring the Social from Across the Disciplines*, eds. Gloria J. Leckie, Lisa M. Given, and John E. Buschman (Santa Barbara, CA: Libraries Unlimited, 2010), 161-72.

transparent.² The primary role for libraries is to facilitate this rational public discourse through encouragement of encounters between citizens embracing a variety of views and preferences by means of securing social communication through equal treatment and free access to, and exchange of, information and knowledge.

The idea of the library as a low-intensive social meeting place and a key institution in local community building continues to be an important trope for public libraries. Since about the turn of the century, this has been extended to include academic libraries as well, with study spaces and cafés gradually replacing bookshelves as students and researchers alike increasingly turn to electronic resources.³ Libraries, as with democracy itself, are formulated around the idea of consensus and rational communication, in itself a delicate matter which requires time and patience. It can only be achieved through education and collective knowledge; educated citizens are, arguably, better equipped to participate in society. It is a classic modernist belief in rational progress channeled through universalist values and politically-neutral institutional structures. These ideas still govern much of librarianship, but societal sentiments have changed over the course of the last couple of decades into a devotion to speed and egotism, with deep consequences for relations between individuals and the disposition of social institutions. This has changed the fundamentals of democracy, leaving

---

2. Jürgen Habermas, *The Theory of Communicative Action, Volume 1: Reason and the Rationalization of Society* (London: Heinemann, 1984).

3. Ragnar Audunson, "The Public Library as a Meeting Place in a Multicultural and Digital Context: The Necessity of Low-Intensive Meeting-Places," *Journal of Documentation* 61 no. 3 (2005): 429-41.

its institutional structures in a constant tension between legitimacy and identity. In the case of librarianship, the more legitimacy is sought, for instance by adapting to perceived user needs or perceived expectations from patrons, the harder it gets to uphold a stable identity for the profession and the institution—and vice versa.

This tension between legitimacy and identity is interesting, as the moral dimension of librarianship firmly relies on the stability and social universalism of liberal democracy. Legitimacy is gained through identity. Challenges facing libraries in various parts of the world differ, but essentially the various shapes of librarianship concur in the struggle for free and equal access to information and knowledge, and the advancement of digitization paired with a strong and substantiated belief in the value of reading and learning. As the International Federation of Library Associations and Institutions (IFLA) currently is working towards a global library strategy, due in 2019, we can expect these values to be formulated in relation to a global development which is by no means one-dimensional. While some parts of the world struggle to define and implement democratic ideals and institutions, others have well-established democratic institutions now challenged by forces which do not necessarily accept them. Examples of the latter can be found today in the populist movements gaining prominence in many European Union countries, as well as in the USA. The lack of regard and value often given to librarianship in these new political environments increasingly creates both practical and normative pressure on librarians; it is thus necessary to maintain a clear mind and an ability to connect to the core values of the profession.

Allow me to make only a brief digression regarding the problem of information as such in this context—I will return to it again later on. It is necessary to comment upon this in light of the development which increasingly connects information with the priorities of the for-profit information industry. This has become *legio* (in the sense of being customary or praxis) today in the general mix-up between economic and democratic values, both within the field of scholarly communication and in the more open area of social media and news distribution. In an analysis of the underlying assumptions about the relation between information and democracy, Brenda Dervin concludes that democracy requires a definition of "good" information as "that which is most isomorphic to reality."[4] In a post-modern, post-welfare, neoliberal social construct characterized by ceaseless disruption and devoid of stable practices and values, the recognition of others must find forms that have the ability to develop beyond the ideal of rational communication in the public sphere. How to maintain a relevant information environment is a crucial problem which is only in part related to the common moral ground of the world's libraries; it more acutely presents itself as a reality for professionals having to deal with the multitude of views and positions ideally displayed through the collections and search tools of libraries. Dervin pertinently defines the problem, stating that "[we] must find a way to think of diversity of views as a step toward never-reachable ontological completeness and as a step away from the tyranny of epistemological completeness."[5] This

---

4. Brenda Dervin, "Information <–>Democracy: An Examination of Underlying Assumptions," *Journal of the American Society for Information Science* 45, no. 6 (1994): 378.

5. Dervin, "Information <–> Democracy," 382.

is indeed a crucial point, and one that has severe practical consequences for the understanding of information behavior as well as the role of libraries of various kinds, in that it stakes out a way to avoid the problem of authoritarian relativism present today. This tends to move away from the "traditional" post-modern notion that everything is interpretation, towards a stand which stresses a non-reciprocal position of one's own interpretation of a specific situation, issue, or general worldview, thus formulating it as absolute (Dervin's "epistemological completeness"). Such "truths" often tend to be advocated through social media hearsay, emotional reactions, or deeply-rooted prejudice, legitimized by an information environment which allows for individuals as well as organizations to deviate from agreed upon rules of behavior in legitimate public discourse. As such, a relativism of the absolute rules out the possibility of the recognition of the other, and a new social position for librarians has to be formulated as well as a new consciousness of the character of open political debate. Both require free and equal access to "good information" as a result of high-quality library services. One way of finding tools for such work is by turning to normative social theory.

I will here point to two such theories which are notably under-developed in the frameworks of librarianship and Library and Information Science: the theory of recognition and the theory of agonistic pluralism. One reason for their scarce use in our field is perhaps due to the fact that both can be seen as opposing the consensus-driven democratic model which is so much connected to librarianship and libraries in society, however not in an epistemological completeness way. Instead, they analyze legitimate conflict as a necessary part of democratic development.

## To Recognize the Other

The concept of recognition has been elaborated upon by German sociologist Axel Honneth, in a social theory carved out of the tradition of the Frankfurt School.[6] It opposes, or at least furthers, Habermas' theory of communicative action, resulting from a rational consensus-oriented public discourse. What Honneth does is create an analytical framework that instead places social conflict at the center of interest.[7] In today's society where striving for uniform enlightenment and communicative consensus has been made obsolete in its original sense by social and technological development, it sometimes becomes more relevant to characterize social relations in terms of conflict. In doing so, the ability to recognize the other is a moral position as well as an identity-confirming one in any given attempt to establish a functioning public discourse. Honneth emphasizes the need for a normative analytic position. Social patterns of conflict may change, but they do not disappear—examples of this include gender inequality, normative whiteness, and (neo)nationalism. We may think of this in terms of how librarianship is defined as normative, political, or democratic in a sense relating to a rationality suggesting that educated citizens are better equipped to foster a democratic, rational public spirit if only given a fair chance. Libraries are, in such a scenario, valid in the wake of democracy but the challenges they have faced in many countries during the last few decades

---

6. Joel Anderson, "Situating Axel Honneth in the Frankfurt School Tradition," in *Axel Honneth: Critical Essays. With a Reply by Axel Honneth*, ed, Danielle Petherbridge (Leiden: Brill, 2011), 31-57.

7. Axel Honneth, *The Struggle for Recognition: The Moral Grammar of Social Conflicts* (Cambridge, UK: Polity Press, 1995).

have created a need for new ideals for both librarianship and education.

Honneth speaks of recognition on three levels: individual, legal, and social. While individual recognition focuses on intimate personal relations and social recognition denotes various collective identities and groups, the legal level refers back to social universals, such as the UN Declaration of Human Rights or constitutional legislation stipulating both rights and responsibilities of the individual citizen. Recognition thus becomes a question of not only politics, but of ethics as well. In order to create rules and limits for a public discourse that can claim legitimacy, in our case for instance through library legislation, recognition of the other must be there first. Furthermore, it has to be accepted by all parts of society. Social pathologies emerge when recognition is not accepted as a prerequisite for public debate, and there are numerous examples of this all over the western world today, most notably perhaps in the rise of neo-nationalism in Europe and the USA. Brexit, Donald Trump's aim of building a wall along the southern US border, and the radical shift in attitude toward non-European refugees and immigrants in the Scandinavian countries. These all bear the same mark: that of a conscious denial of recognition of not just specific groups of people who have not yet come to these countries, but also towards people who have lived there for a long time, perhaps their whole lives, albeit belonging to an ethnic or national minority. This denial is justified by an often vague idea of what it means to be of a certain nationality.

Interestingly enough, this *Zeitgeist* also affects social-democracy, once dedicated to recognition in a sense close to Honneth's but now closing borders and establishing migration policies and a level of restriction that would have been unthinkable only a few years ago. Such pathologies of identity in politics can be seen not only on the social level, but also on the legal level, where human universal values such as those formulated by the United Nations have come under increased scrutiny. This insecurity spills over to librarianship as well. In Sweden, the nationalist party *Sverigedemokraterna* has recently suggested in parliament an adjustment to the current Library Act that would make the services of publicly-funded libraries only available to Swedish citizens, and that would eliminate from the Act the current law-bound priorities for public libraries to work with people with a mother tongue other than Swedish.[8] It's important to know that *Sverigedemokraterna* is not a political fringe movement anymore; founded in neo-Nazi circles in the early 1990s, it is now the third-largest political party in the country, with 17% of the votes in the 2018 parliamentary election. When recognition written into legislation is suddenly no longer accepted by a growing part of the population, social pathologies need to be analyzed on all levels. In order to develop a society on the established basis of democracy, issues of recognition must be addressed, not as a goal in itself, but in order to make it possible to create an ethical foundation for legitimate communicative action. It becomes necessary to accept conflict as a fundamental part of democracy.

In a society where political forces increasingly use social media and various forms of news manipulation to encourage denial of recognition of the other, and at the same time managerial ideals of public institutions avoid taking social conflict into account, what are the consequences for

---

8. Aron Emilsson, Angelika Bengtsson, Sara-Lena Bjälkö and Cassandra Sundin, "Biblioteksfrågor," *Motion till riksdagen* 2016/17: 2208.

librarianship? Nanna Kann-Christensen and Jack Andersen suggest nothing less than rethinking the democratic mission of librarianship. It is no longer sufficient to offer information on a socially equal basis or based on an idea of "good" literature and information—the very focus of text-based media is in itself class dependent and a collective identity marker, and it is an old truth that you are treated "more equal" the more librarian-like you appear when you enter the library.[9] Instead, they insist on the need to shift focus to the recognition of the user on a deeper level:

> Libraries must be reconsidered in such a way that different social groups feel that libraries address their life conditions and human identities. The challenge is to find out where, when and with what means different forms of recognition in different spheres are articulated and how libraries may fit in there.[10]

How this should done is, however, a delicate matter as "[t]he library of recognition works on the borderline between customer satisfaction and the library's normative offers and grounding."[11] One example of how this balance has been made successfully is the work of local libraries in Sweden during, and in the aftermath of, the historically large stream of refugees, primarily from war-torn Syria, who made their way to northern Europe in the fall of 2015. By not only

---

9. Dave Muddiman, Shiraz Durani, John Pateman, Martin Dutch, Rebecca Linley and John Vincent, "Open to All? The Public Library and Social Exclusion: Executive Summary," *New Library World* 102, no. 4/5 (2001): 154-8.

10. Nanna Kann-Christensen and Jack Andersen, "Developing the Library: Between Efficiency, Accountability and Forms of Recognition," *Journal of Documentation* 65 no. 2, (2009): 220.

11. Kann-Christensen and Andersen, 220.

identifying the immediate information needs of refugees in a broad sense, a process well analyzed by Library and Information Science research,[12] but setting an example of both legal and social recognition, often in small rural communities where groups of refugees were bussed and placed in shelters, public libraries proved themselves crucial in the management of social inclusion. This was done in a situation where the sheer number of people coming in paralyzed much of the national immigration authorities and border control system. Not only did public libraries provide a place of civility, they also functioned as low-intensive meeting-places where refugees were met on the same terms as the ordinary local library user. The ethos of the profession proved stronger than the need for predictability and accountability to the new public management governance by which they are bound. The ability to swiftly adapt to a situation characterized by deep human need drew attention and praise from across the public sphere in Sweden. It did, however, also lead to some unexpected consequences, such as that authorities who could not handle certain legal and other immigration-related issues commanded refugees to go to the library and get them sorted out there. Thus, a number of activities well beyond what could reasonably be considered part of professional librarianship had to be dealt with. But dealt with they were. Another consequence was that the organized political far

---

12. Andreas Vårheim, "Trust and the Role of the Public Library in the Integration of Refugees: The Case of a Northern Norwegian City," *Journal of Librarianship and Information Science 46, no.*1 (2014): 62-9; Annemaree Lloyd, "Researching Fractured (Information) Landscapes: Implications for Library and Information Science Researchers Undertaking Research with Refugees and Forced Migration Studies," *Journal of Documentation 73*, no. 1 (2017): 1-15.

right and various nationalist movements started to demand wider access to library services by means of acquisition of literature and newspapers hostile to immigration and Islam, a development which put attention on an issue different from, but closely related to recognition—the limits of legitimacy in public discourse.

In the late 2010s, free speech and the right to express your opinions and views in public debate has once again become a sensitive issue. The social pathologies pointed out by Honneth permeate all parts of public discourse. Traditional media is under scrutiny, public service is being questioned, and alternative media is gradually becoming the main information source for an increasing number of citizens. In many ways this was the promise of the internet as it made its way into people's homes and electronic devices. Now we see how rapid and un-reflexive development of communication technology did not (only) create a new harmonious climate of free discourse, but also an environment where social media and alternative news outlets turn out to be severe problems for civil public debate, which is so crucial for the political and moral structure of democracy. Social media is definitely part of the problem, perhaps even part of the root system of the current political instability and societal nervousness, but it is by no means the only one. Just as important is that institutions, not least political ones, are crumbling under the pressure of a marketplace which simply moves much faster than is possible for democratic structures to handle. The public sector has been forced into adapting its missions and managerial forms in correlation with private sector structures, a process which does not work very well in most cases. The implementation of New Public Management ideals creates a need for many organizations and institutions to adapt to an economically defined re-writing of not only their system of leadership and accountancy, but also of their place in the general division of labor in society. A telling example, which I will return to at length, is the transformation of the structure of decision-making in universities, where arenas for traditional collegial influence over faculties is eliminated and replaced by hierarchical organization models with few levels of executive decision-making. This leads to a concentration of power and the increased importance of administrative priorities over those which are more traditionally academic.

This transformation is easy enough to see, to oppose, and to criticize (as many have done), but it is extremely hard to resist. One reason for this is one which is seldom discussed: that the new public management institutions are constructed in a way which is dependent on uniformity and conformity rather than diversity, on consensus rather than debate. To question and oppose the development of new managerial forms is regarded as a disturbance. This may seem almost like a paradox in the light of general social development—but, why? Well, simply put, as public institutions transform into having managerial structures and practices in line with those of private enterprises, they also subscribe to the underlying goal of economic growth. This is founded upon a logic which cannot really be questioned, because it is not defined in political or ideological terms, but rather in terms of claimed natural consequence and neutral facts. Based on such claims, organizational loyalty is then built. One visible result is the organizational behaviorism of contemporary librarianship, adapting initiatives and practices to perceived user needs, a position developed in close correlation to Library and Information Science research as well, in what Finnish scholar

Vesa Suominen speaks of as "userism."[13] It is not by accident that it is hard to come by ideological analyses by advocates of neoliberalism—most of them do not see ideology, but instead view what emerges as a natural consequence of the demise of ideologies.[14] Should we be surprised? Well, perhaps not anymore; we know these mechanisms all too well and new public management can hardly be regarded as "new" anymore, but was there ever a point? As so often when it comes to matters such as these, it depends on to whom you choose to listen. Like it or loathe it, Karl Marx and Friedrich Engels pointed to this development with pertinence in their *Communist Manifesto* back in 1848.[15]

But who can question the need for accountability and evaluation? It is without doubt reasonable to create awareness of how the public's tax money is being spent and hold responsible those who misuse it. Then again, as the system of evaluation grows, it at some point becomes a control instrument for not just the easily justified question of how money is being used, but of job performance of individuals. In an environment where emphasis is put on individual performance in a competitive situation, the individual

---

13. Vesa Suominen, *About and on Behalf of Sriptum Est: The Literary, Bibliographic and Educational Rationality sui generis of the Library and Librarianship on the Top of What literature has Produced* (Oulu, Finland: University of Oulu, 2016): 69-75.

14. David Harvey, *A Brief History of Neoliberalism* (Oxford: Oxford University Press, 2005), 39-63.

15. Karl Marx and Friedrich Engels, *The Communist Manifesto* (London: Penguin, 1848/2015); see also Yanis Varoufakis, "Marx Predicted our Present Crisis—and Points the Way Out," *The Guardian*, 20 April 2018.

worker—whether a social worker, librarian, or university lecturer—will not be able to act in a way opposed to the defined mission of the institution, regardless of whether the reason was a clear view of what is needed in terms of professional practice or an open opposition to one's own working conditions. Debate and opposition are classified as logical deviations and for such there is no room. But what happens on a social level when opinions and measures can no longer be formed and taken in relation to a variety of options, to be tested against opposing views or scrutinized in public debate with rules and boundaries perceived as legitimate by the participants? That public organizations morph into shapes of conformity does not mean that the people who are affected by their practices don't have a need to express themselves. They just go elsewhere to do so. This is a potential problem. Where no consensus about limits and rules for discussion are present, new kinds of authorities find their ground: hate speech gets confused with freedom of expression, established knowledge gets confused with hoaxes and conspiracies. As the global political system has developed in a way that depends on conformity rather than the tension between democratic conflict and consensus, arenas outside of those agreed upon as legitimate (parliamentary debate, political parties, organized discussions, quality media) appear and have no real boundaries. How then does this affect librarianship? Let us approach this question from a different angle, looking at how the basis of democracy may be formulated by law, the ultimate way of defining the character and limits of public debate and discourse, illustrated here by the example of the Swedish constitution.

## Example: The Library Act of Sweden

Sweden has had rules about how to keep it together as a nation since the early 14th century and a "proper" constitution has been in place since 1634. The Swedish National Day on June 6th commemorates two separate events, both of which took place on this date: the coronation of King Gustav Vasa in 1523 and, more importantly, the signing of the immediate precursor to the current constitution in 1809. That original version of the constitution was in effect until 1974, when it was revised into the current version. The two perhaps most important consequences of the revised constitution were the transformation of the royal throne into a purely ceremonial function and the final abolishment of the death penalty—the last execution in Sweden had taken place in 1910. Today, the Swedish constitution consists of four so-called fundamental laws:

- The Instrument of Government, formulating the division of power,
- The Act of Succession, regulating who is Head of State,
- The Freedom of the Press Act—the oldest law of its kind in the world, protecting free press and print since 1765, and
- The Fundamental Law on Freedom of Expression.

Two of these relate directly to the practice of librarianship. The Freedom of the Press Act not only stipulates the right to produce independent journalism and printed works, it is also closely tied to the Duty Shipping Act of 1661. This stipulates the delivery of all printed material in Sweden to the Royal

Library, which is the National Library of Sweden, directly from the printers, not from the publishers. Since 2013, this act also covers the collection of Swedish websites and digital publications. Along with that, the Fundamental Law on Freedom of Expression provides the point of departure for the mission of librarianship as stipulated in the Library Act, first signed in 1996 and updated to its current version in 2013.

The first of the fundamental laws in the Swedish constitution, The Instrument of Government, has an opening paragraph which is worth quoting in full:

> §1: All public power emanates from the people. The Swedish popular government is built upon freedom of expression and upon the general and equal right to vote. Is is manifested through representative and parliamentary governance and through regional autonomy. Public power is executed under the law.[16]

Freedom of expression is here formulated as the most significant feature of democracy, followed by the right to vote. In its second paragraph, The Instrument of Government formulates the aim of all public institutions and services:

> §2: Public power should be executed with respect for all people's equal value and the freedom and dignity of the individual. The personal, economic, and cultural welfare of the individual should be the fundamental mission of public service. Public service should especially secure the right to work, housing, and education and to strive for social care and security as well as healthy living conditions.[17]

---

16. Svensk författningssamling 1974:152. http://www.riksdagen.se/sv/dokument-lagar/dokument/svensk-forfattningssamling/kungorelse-1974152-om-beslutad-ny-regeringsform_sfs-1974-152.

17. Svensk författningssamling 1974:152.

The Swedish constitution emphasizes that the freedom and dignity of the individual is to be defined in personal (integrity), economic (security), *and* cultural (civility) welfare. Cultural welfare is not something which can be neglected as less important than, for instance, the right to economic security. Nor is it negotiable in the competition for public funding. This is also a point where the Library Act taps into the constitution. Its second paragraph, the so-called "mission paragraph", reads as follows:

> §2: Libraries included in the public library system [that is, all tax-funded libraries] shall work for the development of democratic society and freedom of expression. Libraries included in the public library system shall advance the standing of literature and interest in civility, enlightenment, education, and research, as well as other cultural activities. Library activity shall be available for all.[18]

What we see here is a direct mirroring of the expressions in the opening paragraph of the constitution. This is no soft, be-nice-to-everybody liberal democratic play—this is hard democracy to the core, and libraries are at the center of it. The referred-to public library system includes, apart from public libraries as such, academic libraries, school libraries, regional library activities, national book deposits, and "other publicly funded library activity." One of the most important parts of the Act is the definition of the groups to be prioritized by the publicly funded library system: disabled persons, national minorities, and people with a mother-tongue other than Swedish. This is recognition in practice on both social and legal levels, as well as a way to create a legitimate space for

---

18. Svensk författningssamling 2013:801. The Swedish term translated here as "civility," is "bildning" or *Bildung*, as discussed in the previous chapter.

negotiating social conflict and debate. In Swedish legislation, libraries are put at the center of deliberative democratic development, positioned explicitly to fulfill the aims of the opening paragraph of the constitution. There is only one problem: there is no mention of librarians.

The question of competence among those who work in and lead libraries, specifically public libraries, is a sensitive one. Looking at legislation in other Nordic countries, we find a clear ambivalence there as well towards a Library and Information Science-based competence structure. The Norwegian Library Act states that leaders of public libraries are required to have a Library and Information Science degree, but, and this is of course important, exceptions can be made in accordance with local demands.[19] The Library Act of Finland formulates its demand for Library and Information Science competence as such: the library should have "sufficient numbers of employees with degrees within the library and information field, and sufficient numbers of others employed."[20] In short, competence is open for negotiation. These examples are unique in relation to their respective administrative traditions, but they represent three of the most developed countries in the world when it comes to librarianship; in the case of how competencies are formulated, we find similar situations in many other countries as well. There are at least three things which matter in this legal indecisiveness concerning librarianship as the obvious profession for running and developing libraries: the

---

19. Lovdata. Lov om Folkebibliotek. https://lovdata.no/dokument/NL/lov/1985-12-20-108#KAPITTEL_1.

20. Finlex. Lag om allmänna bibliotek, 29.12.2016/1492. https://www.finlex.fi/sv/laki/ajantasa/2016/20161492.

question of legitimacy, how to deal with a normative mission, and challenges for education.

## *Legislative Ambiguity*

The library institution receives its prime legitimacy through the professional conduct and authority of librarians in relation to the users of the library. If librarians are not there, others will claim that authority on their own behalf. We see this in everything from the drastic cuts to libraries in the UK, to the use of senior citizens and others to replace librarians during certain operating hours, to the increased use of staff-less libraries.[21] Prioritization of activities which only with utmost difficulty can be fit into the democratic sentiment of legislation may suddenly gain legitimacy. One such example can be found in my own hometown, Växjö in southeast Sweden, whose administrative leadership recently ordered the city public library to embark on an expensive campaign to prioritize e-sport in the library's facilities and, more importantly, within its budget.[22] E-sport is certainly up-and-coming in limited (mostly male) groups among the young, but can it fit into the priorities made clear in the Library Act? Hardly. Engaging in e-sport should of course be an option for anyone interested, but it cannot be legitimized as democratically necessary, and certainly not at the expense of more fundamental library activities. The problem from a professional perspective is that there are very few means that can be used to stop initiatives such as this. It is emblematic of all regulation surrounding the practice of librarianship

---

21. Carl Gustav Johannsen, *Staff-Less Libraries: Innovative Staff Design* (Oxford, UK: Chandos, 2017).

22. Växjö City Library. https://bibliotek.vaxjo.se/sv_SE/web/arena/kodoteket.

that neither legislation nor professional ethics are possible to examine legally. Robert Hauptmann laments this situation in his book *Ethics and Librarianship*, in which he discusses ethical codes and guidelines for professional conduct as tools for meeting attempts to deviate from core practices of the profession. He also points to the other end of this problem, the possibility of holding professionals accountable for their actions (or non-actions) in relation to not just economic performance but mission fulfilment.[23] Should librarians refuse to implement e-sport without getting sufficient additional funds, if this activity is demanded from forces outside the professional realm? Could they? I will not attempt to answer this here, but it seems clear that given the non-existence of a defined authoritative competence for running the library, the law provides at best guidelines for priorities but hardly any real obligations that can direct a concrete response.

The second problem with ambiguity concerning professional governance of libraries is that legislation tends to be highly normative. The Swedish example stipulates not only what practices but also what groups of people should be prioritized. To work for the advancement of first civility and enlightenment, and then education and research, is a clear indication of the non-instrumental mission of librarianship; this is also the case for those types of libraries that we usually connect with formal, instrumental learning processes such as school libraries and university libraries. This priority clearly denotes the foundation of the democratic welfare state before the arrival of neoliberal instrumentalism.

---

23. Robert Hauptman, *Ethics and Librarianship* (Jefferson, NC: McFarland, 2002), 10-11.

Libraries are not part of the educational system, but mean to contribute to it in a complementary way that is important for democratic participation. This is a strong sentiment which more often than not collides with the administrative ideals of today. The prioritization of groups such as national minorities, indigenous peoples, and immigrants emphasizes the recognition of the other, and is a natural consequence of the constitution's fundamental laws. However, while these formulations are as clear as they are deliberative, it is difficult to see who is positioned to uphold them. The undefined professional basis for libraries puts them in a situation stuck between two ideals: on the one hand, the mission formulated in the Library Act; on the other, the often far more regulative economic and administrative practices of the local city or community governance or a mother-institution such as a university. As economy, performance, and accountability tend to take precedence over any professional core practice (we see this in, for instance, the medical professions as well), a non-binding Library Act without a strong professional mandate to guard it, is sure to fall prey to challenges.

This leads us to the third aspect of legislative ambiguity, which concerns education. If legislation dismisses the value of professional judgment, how should the preparation of future librarians be formulated within the university? There is no "library academy" in the sense of there being in many countries a "police academy"; there is no Hippocratic oath which holds the profession together no matter within what institutional setting the individual librarian works. There is only tradition. This tradition fits well into the formulations of the Swedish legislation, and perhaps even more so into the radical formulation of the Norwegian Public Library Law, which states that "[p]ublic libraries shall be an autonomous meeting-place and arena for public discourse and debate."[24] However, Library and Information Science has long had difficulties in handling tradition and in incorporating this not only normative, but emancipatory, perspective in its formulations of what it means to be a librarian. This can be directly linked to the position of professional tradition. The formulation of any profession, and librarianship is no exception, tends to be a pronouncement of existing practices, developed into a form which may gain authority in relation to other close or similar practices or competences. It is natural to think that this connection would be made in Library and Information Science, as the academic discipline has its prime legitimacy in established practices of librarianship whether defined as the "enduring values" of Michael Gorman,[25] André Cosette's "philosophy of librarianship,"[26] or Suzanne Briet's "cultural technique" of documentation.[27] However, references to its various professional practices over time can be considered disturbingly conservative or even obsolete, as the information field finds itself captured in a cult of The

---

24. Lovdata. Lov om Folkebibliotek. https://lovdata.no/dokument/NL/lov/1985-12-20-108#KAPITTEL_1.

25. Michael Gorman, *Our Enduring Values: Librarianship in the 21st Century* (Chicago: American Library Association, 2002).

26. André Cosette, *Humanism and Libraries: An Essay on the Philosophy of Librarianship* (Duluth, MN: Library Juice Press, 1976/2009).

27. Suzanne Briet, *What is Documentation? English Translation of the Classic French Text,* translated and edited by Ronald E. Day and Laurent Martinet (Lanham, MD: Scarecrow Press, 1951/2006). See also Ronald E. Day, "Tropes, History and Ethics in Professional Discourse and Information Science," *Journal of the American Society for Information Science* 51, no. 5 (2000): 469-75.

New. That established "traditional" practices can be seen in the light of democracy, and even of social emancipation, is still being viewed as radical. Without them, however, other interests take precedence: interests that are often neither benevolent towards, nor conceived as beneficiaries of, the ideological tensions and demands that constitute the very basis of democracy. Once again, as it happens, this comes down to the handling of recognition and social conflict within the library and information field. In order to manage this, a strong foundation is needed. There is, however, no doubt that the discipline has the potential to drive developments which include more emancipatory readings of central concepts and theories.

## *Defining Library Practice from Democratic Conflict*

Swedish scholar Johanna Rivano Eckerdal provides a reading of the concepts of "library" and "information literacy" which confirms not only the legitimacy extended by these examples of library legislation, but the connection between the mission and authority of the institution and the professional practices of librarians.[28] In a similar way to how Kann-Christensen and Andersen suggested a redefinition of the social role of libraries by bringing the concept of recognition into the center, Rivano Eckerdal suggests an evolved reading of library services in terms of "agonistic pluralism," a concept developed by Belgian sociologist Chantal Mouffe.[29]

---

28. Johanna Rivano Eckerdal, "Libraries, Democracy, Information, and Citizenship: An Agonistic Reading of Central Library and Information Studies' Concepts," *Journal of Documentation* 73 no. 5 (2017): 1010-33.

29. Chantal Mouffe, *The Democratic Paradox* (London: Verso, 2000) and Chantal Mouffe, *On the Political* (Abingdon, UK: Routledge, 2005). See

Perhaps Mouffe's most important point is that conflict is the very substance of democracy. Her writings construct a radical agenda, finding a discrepancy between two basic forms of political understanding: one liberal, emphasizing the individual and its relation to universal human rights; and one democratic, with popular sovereignty, equality, and a common understanding, perhaps even identification, between the public institution (the governing) and the people (the governed) as the center of interest. The latter provides legitimate room for ideological tension within institutional practices, while the former places the individual above the institutional structures of democracy. As the liberal political understanding dominates today in the form of neoliberal hegemony, tension exists in relation to democratic understanding, something which Mouffe defines as a democratic paradox. As patterns of conflict have gone from being grounded in formal categories such as "left" and "right" to instead being formulated in moral terms of "good" and "bad," the conditions for political practice and discourse have changed. Values such as equality, diversity, and democratic transparency are devalued as they are found to be in opposition to individual freedom in line with the economically (thus non-politically) defined worldview of neoliberalism.

Agonistic struggle is a way of balancing the us-and-them dichotomy in society which inevitably emerges if moral definitions of political problems are allowed to dominate.

---

also Joacim Hansson, "Chantal Mouffe's Theory of Agonistic Pluralism and Its Relevance for Library and Information Science Research" in *Critical Theory for Library and Information Science: Exploring the Social from across the Disciplines*, eds. Gloria J. Leckie, Lisa M. Given, and John E. Buschman (Santa Barbara, CA: Libraries Unlimited, 2010), 249-57.

Instead, a radical alternative is to create democratic institutions within which a legitimate conflict of ideas and practices can take place. If the political goal is to reach consensus, politics are reduced to administration and the symbolic room opens up for fringe movements which may gain momentum as the moral definition of "bad" can easily turn towards the institutions themselves. As neoliberalism has taken its hold over the European political landscape, this is exactly what is happening. The consensus model which is implemented in the governing bodies of the EU has led to the rise of far-right populism and the re-emergence of fascist parties in many of its member states, including Italy, Hungary, Denmark, Sweden, Finland, the Netherlands, and France. This stalemate of established democratic institutions can also be found in regional and national politics in individual countries regardless of the EU, as governing coalitions strive for consensus to secure economic growth instead of encouraging agonism within the governing construct. This has provided an opportunity for fringe movements to define what they see as moral conflicts between an "us" (i.e., nationals) and a "them" (i.e., immigrants) or between the "people" and the "elite," with the elite representing the democratic institutions. The way to meet this development, according to Mouffe, is to accept that there is no one way of organizing society or to address societal challenges—there are always several. By allowing for this fundamental recognition of the other, and creating symbolic as well as institutional space to exercise this recognition in political struggle, she manages to formulate a radical democratic theory which emphasizes the role of institutions as necessary to secure democratic development as a kind of counter-culture against the neoliberal hegemony.

She formulates recognition in a significantly different manner from Honneth; however, she still ends up in a similar place.

Where Honneth sees recognition as a necessary moral basis of democracy, and a necessary prerequisite for democratic communicative action to occur, Mouffe tries to tame the moral impetus and instead points to the necessity of active, conflict-framing institutions based on regulation and agreed-upon discursive limits. This difference can at least in part be explained by their different theoretical backgrounds: while Honneth forms his theory well within the confines of the Frankfurt School and in direct dialogue with Hegel's early writings, Mouffe fosters a neo-Marxist psychoanalytic line of thought, building on the primacy of structures over that of agents. To Mouffe, democratic development is not defined by studying the relations of individuals, institutions, and society, as in Honneth's three levels; she stays on the institutional level and predicts consequences from institutional practices for viability within society, and through that also for individuals. Bringing them together as a basis for argument in relation to librarianship and library education becomes reasonable when pondering the social character of librarianship. This is true not only in more or less autonomous local public libraries, but also in academic libraries that have a significant influence on the production of scientific communication and the societal dissemination of scientific knowledge.

I have now discussed the social, normative character of librarianship in a way which leads to consequences for developing practices, regardless of what type of library we are dealing with. One of the many people who have brought attention to such consequences is Jonathan Cope, who shows how teaching librarians at universities exercise institutional authority through their student instruction practices.[30] In an essay considering how to confront student intolerance, through an example of "the reconquista student" who advocates xenophobic views in class, he finds that literature on Critical Information Literacy (CIL) generally fails to provide solutions for handling such individuals and situations. As a general consensus of civility and respect for the views of the other can no longer be taken for granted, he argues for an analysis of the situation based on an agonistic view of library instruction:

> [T]he American university exists in a society that is riven by inequality and conflict; therefore what librarians who support the goals of CIL require is a theory of the political that can navigate the tension between standing with social movements and insurgencies for justice on the one hand, and exercising institutional authority to create a pluralist classroom or library on the other.[31]

This is a pertinent formulation of the tension between legitimacy and identity that is necessary to continuously revisit and revise in libraries and librarianship. To be professional is to work in line with the institutional values of the organization, whether library, school, or university, and still maintain the ethos handed down through the traditions of the profession. If this is done well, it creates professional legitimacy in relation to patrons, the public, and, as in Cope's example, students. However, to be professional is also to be conscious of the role of conflict in discussions in the

---

30. Jonathan T. Cope, "The Reconquista Student: Critical Information Literacy, Civics, and Confronting Student Intolerance," *Communications in Information Literacy* 11, no. 2 (2017): 264-82.

31. Cope, 274-5.

public sphere, whether a city square, a town hall rally, or in the classroom or the library at a university. If a user or a student vents racist views, misogyny, or a rhetorical position based on the lack of recognition of underprivileged groups or individuals, staying "neutral" is not an option. Instead, professional identity and integrity is then shown through an advocacy for the recognition of the other as well the initiation and pursuit of a discussion where the aim is not to eliminate the other, but to debate with respect—to create a political "pluriverse." Professionalism does not, however, consist of addressing one's own views on a situation, but in internalizing the given institutional authority into it, so that the library as such sets the limits for what Honneth speaks of as the moral grammar of social conflict. Rivano Eckerdal summarizes the relation between legislation, institutional authority, and individual ethics well by stating: "[w]hen the democratic aim is interpreted agonistically, libraries are important places for producing counter-hegemonies and enabling equality of the less privileged."[32]

John Buschman has pointed out that scholarly debate, as well as empirical evidence focusing the democratic meaning and function of libraries, is scarce, but my impression is that this has improved in the last decade, not least with the emergence of critical information literacy and critical knowledge organization.[33] Recent developments in the political state of many western societies also prompts the

---

32. Rivano Eckerdal, "Libraries, Democracy, Information, and Citizenship," 1022.

33. John Buschman, "Democratic Theory in Library and Information Science: Toward an Emendation," *Journal of the American Association for Information Science and Technology* 58, no.10 (2007): 1483-6.

relevance of perspectives such as those exemplified here. The understanding of the prerequisites for democratic participation in political environments much more hostile to deliberative democratic ideals than most librarians are used to needs to be discussed. The rise of authoritarianism on both sides of the Atlantic provides new challenges for libraries of all sorts. In most European countries, libraries and the legitimacy of librarianship is threatened on several levels. Sweden, as it happens, remains an exception with a recently adopted national library strategy[34] which significantly strengthens the entire interconnected library system. I do, however, hesitate to mention this as sustainable. There are overall three main obstacles for library development today: economic cutbacks, political pressure, and ambiguity concerning the value and status of professional librarianship.

Economic cutbacks in libraries are more or less ubiquitous in the EU, and we see it to various degrees in the USA as well. The pursuit of legitimacy leads to activities and managerial forms that meet perceived demands of patrons and users, although such adaptability runs the risk of stretching too far. Administrative angst and nervousness often lead libraries astray into initiatives and priorities that have nothing to do with the basic democratic or emancipatory mission of the library, be it through investments in e-sport or an increase in operating hours without professional staff.

Political pressure takes different forms in different countries. The rise of political right-wing populism has put the consensus-oriented model for the library as a democratic institution to test, whether it concerns library instruction

---

34. *Demokratins skattkammare: förslag till en nationell biblioteksstrategi* (Stockholm: Kungliga biblioteket, 2019).

practices in increasingly politically-charged universities, serious questioning of the intentions of library acts, or user counter-actions taken to secure "free speech" by demanding that alternative news media be represented in the library's offerings of newspapers in a situation where large numbers of immigrants trigger a discussion on the need for diversity and recognition.

Ambiguity concerning the role and status of professional librarianship, both in the ordinary staffing of libraries and in leadership positions, comes as a result of the two former obstacles. Neoliberal organizations tend to prioritize administrative leadership over that which is executed by experts in the field in which the organization is working. We see it in hospitals where the traditional roles of physicians are held back to the benefit of administrators who turn healthcare into a matter of economics and statistics. We see it also in libraries and universities where the relation between content and value in the organization is replaced through administrative governance suggesting quantitative quality-indicators being the top priority for the organization. Without a strong profession to guard the democratic non-profit values of libraries, there is no one else who will perform this function. I maintain that this is the principal threat to libraries, and it is directly linked to the hegemonic capitalistic mode of production which has been allowed to dominate in western societies for more than three decades. That this seemingly impenetrable system is the largest threat not just to libraries, but to any notion of a "good life" based on knowledge and respect for the other has profound consequences for the way in which we need to develop Library and Information Science; we see a mission rising here, to restore librarianship and to create professionalism as a criterion for both the legitimacy and the identity of the discipline. And, of course, it works both ways. However, this is easier said than done.

It is always important to remember that things could be different than they are. We are closing in on a tipping-point in our political development, where it is no longer viable for librarianship to regard itself as a profession positioned to realize a consensus-based arena of rational communication. Instead the profession, in all types of libraries, needs to move towards a conflict-oriented understanding of its mission and by doing so, foster a way to create room for adversaries to encounter each other in legitimate political struggle. For many librarians, this is most likely an uncomfortable thought. The way to do this must be to let professional discourse build on a strong sentiment of institutional authority, based on legislation and principles of professional ethics; in situations where these conflicts occur, professional ethics should always be the guiding light for the individual librarian. The defense of freedom of information—the right to open knowledge, digital inclusion, and meaningful reading experiences—is not a way to guard a social *status quo* anymore: it is a radical social change impetus. In order to achieve a viable education for this kind of librarianship, Library and Information Science needs to be discussed in relation to the development of universities, and with that as a backdrop engage in a serious discussion on the ideological underpinning of recent developments within the discipline itself, both on an organizational and an epistemological level. The emergence and expansion of the iSchool movement is necessary to address in the same ways as are the libraries in which a majority of its students will end up, regardless of the discipline's efforts to formulate an "iField" detached from institutional and ideological bindings. The question is if Library and Information Science will be able to educate the librarians that society now needs and if not, what could, or should, be done? This concern will now be our guide through the rest of this book. Let me begin by addressing the contemporary university.

*Chapter 3*

## UNIVERSITIES AND THE SPEED OF LIFE

A large part of the previous chapter was devoted to providing examples of analytical approaches that take the understanding of libraries, primarily public ones, and librarianship further into the realm of contemporary politics and societal challenges. A main component of this development is the suggestion to replace a consensus-based view of institutions in democratic development with a more conflict-oriented one. Important aspects of the professional identity of librarians have been built on the assumption that they have promoted democratic ideals and practices in those countries where this particular political system has prevailed. And indeed, they have. Traditionally, these ideals have been handed down between generations of librarians through apprenticeship, but with gradual professionalization, they have been reshaped within Library and Information Science to fit the ideals of higher education as well. These have in turn developed in the tension between autonomous, theory-driven scholarship and the social or economic relevance that has come to dominate educational discourse since at least the early 1960s. At that time, Clark Kerr of Berkeley University introduced his famous idea of the university sector as a "knowledge industry." From then on, it would be easy to claim that there is perhaps no public or semi-public part of society that has implemented the narrative of the neoliberal vision and rewritten its own mission, both epistemologically and organizationally, more elegantly than the university sector. It has created as its product that which to a certain degree defines contemporary society—knowledge. Not, however, as a source of wisdom or as a means for reflection, but as a tool for economic growth. The neoliberal narrative that preaches economic growth as the equivalence of democratic development is today manifested through the ways that universities act and present this product, both locally and on an international level.

## *The Contemporary University: A European Perspective*

Literature on the contemporary university is vast and I will not even attempt to create an overview of it here. There are, however, some elements which recur in the lines of argumentation advocating, as well as opposing, current developments. In his well-balanced book *Accelerating Academia*, to which I will return in a while, Filip Vostal analyzes a particular rhetoric at the base of today's university development: competitiveness and excellence. His point is that rhetorical terms or concepts are never only rhetorical, but find their meaning through implementation. This doesn't even have to be with new concepts, but can instead be a recontextualization that brings new meanings and practices into play. His conclusion is telling:

> Whereas competitiveness-talk imposes a racing modality as an instrument for 'just' distribution of funds, status and competencies, excellence-talk entails an ongoing—and competitive—striving for perfection in multiple internal academic settings. This is not to say that competition for recognition and striving for perfection are new and somehow distinctive aspects of academia….What is perhaps different

and relatively new is the brand of publicly and culturally endorsed competition and the hegemony of excellence that is sustained, promoted and installed with the help of a rhetoric clearly oriented to economism.[1]

Vostal is writing this from a European perspective, and his analysis is based on the relatively recent development of new forms of governance and missions of universities in countries within the EU, primarily in the UK. The European Union project has always been one of securing peace through cultural identity as well as one of economic growth. The restructuring of European higher education institutions into their current form took off with the Sorbonne Declaration on "harmonisation of the architecture of the European higher education system" in 1998, signed by the ministers of education of France, Germany, the UK, and Italy.[2] It consists of two main parts: (1) the aim to promote the mobility of students and teaching staff between universities in these four countries, and (2) the aim to promote a uniform system of qualifications with regard to the needs of the labor market. The following year, the slightly expanded and more pragmatic Bologna Declaration was signed in June 1999 by twenty-nine ministers of education within the EU and its associated countries.[3] The result was the creation of a "higher education

---

1. Filip Vostal, *Accelerating Academia: The Changing Structure of Academic Time* (London: Palgrave-Macmillan, 2016), 113.

2. *Sorbonne Joint Declaration: Joint Declaration on the Harmonisation of the Architecture of the European Higher Education System, Paris, the Sorbonne 25 May 1998.* https://www.donau-uni.ac.at/imperia/md/content/io/cop034_sorbonne_declaration.pdf.

3. *Bologna Declaration of 19 June 1999: Joint Declaration of the European Ministers of Education.* https://www.eurashe.eu/library/modernising-phe/

area" in Europe. This was in itself not uncontroversial, as any attempt on behalf of the EU to create uniformity runs the risk of indicating steps towards a federation, something which not all countries want. Today that particular question is more or less dead but the education sector is important both for federalists and those advocating a less intrusive union. The consequence of the Bologna Declaration has been far-reaching on a practical level in that it divides higher education into two "main cycles": one undergraduate and one graduate, where the latter sets criteria for masters and Ph.D. exams, building on three-year bachelor degrees. As these degrees are uniform, comparable, and even commutable between countries, the ambition of the Sorbonne Declaration has in a way been fulfilled. The levels of degrees are explicitly set up in relation to the needs of the surrounding society, with employability being the main goal at the undergraduate (bachelor) level. This means that higher education in Europe has become the subject of political influence in a way previously unseen. As new political opportunities appeared, not least through the encouragement of uniform quality assessment systems, implementation of the Bologna Declaration has been systematically paired with the idea of broadened admittance to university programs, motivated partly by democratic and diversity-driven arguments, but more importantly by economic ones. Universities were transformed into tools with which to tackle unemployment, and they prove to be a significant part in what is sometimes referred to in EU documentation as the "productivity puzzle." But, was this really the intent?

---

Bologna_1999_Bologna-Declaration.pdf.

European higher education has, since the mid-1800s, been influenced by the ideals of the German humanist Wilhelm von Humboldt, who envisioned the university as an institution where the needs of the human spirit should be cultivated through exploration, inquiry, judgement, meditation, analysis, and the desire to understand the world. The years that a person spends in a university should sharpen the senses and the ability to function in a society built on civility and respect. The idea is that universities sustain external ease and internal pressure—the quest to reflect upon and understand society and the natural world should be given a sanctuary, freed from the demands of the surrounding environment. Within academia, the Bologna Declaration is generally considered to have changed this into what Swedish social anthropologist Torbjörn Friberg describes as an "inversion of ideals."[4] He argues that although the consequences of the Bologna Declaration have been profound, the ideals of Humboldt are still considered the norm for academic work and identity among many scholars, while the more practical Bologna ideals represent a kind of deviance from this. This leads to a string of conflicts, amongst the most prominent being the increased expectation for faculty to facilitate academic work for students who tend to position themselves as, on the one hand, customers who expect to pass courses and graduate from programs, and on the other hand as victims—as when teachers impose traditional academic demands such as reading and writing abilities. The way for academics to

---

4. Torbjörn Friberg, "Akademiska subjekt och politisk-ekonomiska processer" in *Den högre utbildningen: ett fält av marknad och politik*, eds. Daniel Ankaroo and Torbjörn Friberg (Möklinta: Gidlunds, 2012), 104.

solve this is, according to Friberg, to maintain focus on the bigger picture of the social, political, and economic processes in society. This should also ring true for teaching librarians, as we saw in the example of the "reconquista student" study discussed in the previous chapter.

The Bologna Declaration is a political document, formulated to consolidate the direction initiated by the Sorbonne Declaration and designed to meet the educational requirements of a Europé, characterized by stable economic growth. It can also be seen as a kind of political reply to *the original* Bologna Declaration, the *Magna Charta Universitatum*, formulated for the 900-year anniversary of the Bologna University in 1988. Here, the university sector itself defines its character and contribution to society. It recognizes four fundamental principles guiding European universities: (1) institutional autonomy, (2) an integral connection between teaching and research, (3) academic freedom in research and teaching, and (4) a devotion to universal knowledge. These are all interconnected, but I would like to highlight a few of the formulations found in these principles. The first principle, stating institutional autonomy for universities says, that "to meet the needs of the world around it, its research and teaching must be morally and intellectually independent of all political authority and economic power."[5] The reason for this is that the university "produces, examines, appraises and hands down culture by research and teaching."[6] What culture

---

5. Observatory, *Magna Charta Universitatum* (Bologna: University of Bologna, 1988), http://www.magna-charta.org/magna-charta-universitatum/the-magna-charta-1.

6. Observatory, *Magna Charta Universitatum*, n.p.

are we looking at here? The fourth principle provides at least one answer, and I quote it in its entirety:

> A university is a trustee of the European humanist tradition; its constant care is to attain universal knowledge; to fulfill its vocation it transcends geographical and political frontiers, and affirms the vital needs for different cultures to know and influence each other.[7]

Humanist tradition, universal knowledge, geographical transcendence, intellectual independence, and institutional autonomy—these fundamental principles of contemporary European universities are, when universities formulate them themselves, almost completely in line with Humboldt's ideal of learning. This is a good example of what Friberg means when he claims that this role is seen as the "normal" role of university practice among scholars. This declaration provides significant support for claiming that this is not just a feeling, but that the European scholarly community sees the university, in a very concrete and practical manner, as a Humboldtian institution.

It is important to recognize that the declarations of the late 1990s are political responses to the spirit of the *Magna Charta*. They are a reaction against the idealism of these principles, underscoring that institutional autonomy and the fostering of a humanist tradition are kinds of eccentric luxuries—universities have a role to play in the competitive environment of the knowledge society and this has to be politically initiated and controlled. The latest incarnation of this political reassurance is the effectively promoted "entrepreneurial university."

---

7. *Ibid.*

## Example: The Entrepreneurial University

In the US tradition of higher education, the concept of "the corporate university" has been around for a long time. The combination of different forms of public and private funding options has made connections between universities and external stakeholders natural, and even if we limit our view to the introduction of library education into the university sector in the 1920s, this too proves to be an example of such interconnection. The European situation is somewhat different. The tradition laid out in the *Magna Charta Universitatum* has, in most countries, been confined to the public sphere. The driving force behind the knowledge society as the template for the restructuring of higher education around the latest turn of the century is based on deregulation of economic barriers and globalization. This is a development claiming new roles for universities, much in line with the US model, where the boundaries between the public non-profit motivation for higher education and private for-profit research funding is diminished. This has prompted European universities to come up with a way to institutionalize a new kind of openness in their goals, in order to address "societal challenges" as intended in the Bologna Declaration. This has, however, subjected universities to explicit political pressure and influence, not least in Sweden, where universities perform more or less by means of a client agreement with the government's national research and educational policy. The institutional model that has been created to meet these political demands has become known as "the entrepreneurial university" and is, if nothing else, the final stab in the back of the last few remains of Humboldtian idealism.

As universities have been increasingly set up to deal with the political idea that extended education for more or less every individual is economically beneficial to society and that this benefit is the highest goal of the entire educational system, they have had to come up with an idea for how to create a rhetorical compass by which to navigate through, on the one hand, the complexities of large masses of students, who due to the pressure to "study" often seem to enter universities with low motivation, and on the other hand, the need to compete on the international market of the knowledge economy. The way to do this is to formulate an ideal type of student: the young up-and-coming entrepreneur. An entrepreneur, according to the *Cambridge Dictionary* is "[s]omeone who starts their own business, especially when this involves seeing a new opportunity."[8] Other definitions from other dictionaries and encyclopedias are similar, with some also including the willingness to take risks. So far, so good. The entrepreneurial university is, however, somewhat more complicated to define. In 2012, the European Commission together with the Organisation for Economic Co-operation and Development (OECD) published *A Guiding Framework for Entrepreneurial Universities*.[9] This document is not a benchmarking tool, but rather a checklist to be used by universities that want to label themselves as "entrepreneurial." Instead of defining the entrepreneurial university, it concludes that "there is an invaluable plurality of approaches, inventive, creative and yet practical which distinguish the entrepreneurial style."[10]

---

8. *Cambridge Dictionary* s.v. "entrepreneur," https://dictionary.cambridge.org/dictionary/english/entrepreneur.

9. *A Guiding Framework for Entrepreneurial Universities*, European Commission / OECD, 2012, https://www.oecd.org/site/cfecpr/EC-OECD%20Entrepreneurial%20Universities%20Framework.pdf.

10. *A Guiding Framework for Entrepreneurial Universities*, 2.

This disclaimer is used as a point of departure for inspiring university leaders in "effective management of institutional and cultural change"—and indeed, a cultural change it is. The explicitly political framework of entrepreneurialism introduces a rhetoric into university practice which is unambiguous. From an ideological point of view, we see this in formulations relating to both structural and individual levels. On the structural level, there is an overtly neoliberal tone set, emphasizing for instance that "[o]vercoming bureaucratic barriers is key to entrepreneurship,"[11] and stating that "[u]niversities are entrepreneurial when they are not afraid to maximise their potential, diversify funding sources and reduce their dependency of state/public funding."[12]

This of course comes as no surprise, but it is interesting in that reducing dependency on public funding has a strong symbolic meaning. In Sweden, as in many other European countries, this conflict is not merely between public or private funding, but is just as much between publicly-based funding within universities (internal funding) and funding through national research councils or EU funds (external funding), both categories being part of a massive redistribution system of tax-based research funds. The important idea here is that the quality of research improves if funding is gained through competition. This has led to an industrial-sized ritual of annual application writing, which for many scholars tends to eat up a significant amount of time that could have been used for research. Bureaucratic barriers refer to taxation and the legitimate regulation of commercial enterprises that are used to secure democratic ideals and the integrity of

---

11. *A Guiding Framework for Entrepreneurial Universities*, 5.

12. *A Guiding Framework for Entrepreneurial Universities*, 6.

public institutions. Public funding, tax money, is generally distributed to endeavors which have the political and/or legislative function of upholding certain values of society. In the tradition of European higher education and as seen in the *Magna Charta*, these are: universal knowledge, civility, and a foundation for democratic development, based on the idea that educated citizens can contribute to informed political development—as well as provide the labor market with educated and skilled people. Now, there is of course nothing inherently wrong with encouraging entrepreneurialism. Just as it is possible to argue that democratic values were secured through the construct of social institutions designed for popular governance, which facilitate participation in political decision-making, it can be argued that entrepreneurialism is the key to develop the means and tools for individuals and society as a whole to develop services and material goods which are for the benefit of all. In the same way, the entrepreneurial university is not in itself a problematic institution when it comes to promoting values such as internationalization, increased external relationships, and flexibility in addressing societal changes. Strong institutions usually maintain an isomorph relationship to surrounding environments and social change indeed needs to be addressed by relevant institutional development. Complexity arises when conflicting values appear as one set of fundamental principles are replaced by another within the realm of one and the same institution. In the case of the entrepreneurial university, one such values conflict is seen in the above quote concerning the dismissal of public funding, and another one is the attitude towards, and prioritization of, certain qualities of the people attending and working there. The EU/OECD guiding framework only goes so far as to advise universities to "encourage entrepreneurial behavior" and create "widespread awareness among staff and students of the importance of developing a range of entrepreneurial abilities and skills…" The entrepreneurial university is, basically, down to the individuals who populate it, and making it manifest is, more or less, a matter of pedagogics. This becomes a matter of judgement which is difficult to argue for in times when mass education is implemented as a way of securing economic growth, even if the relation between long undergraduate university programs and a stronger labor market or more enlightened individuals have been difficult to prove. Instead, and this might seem like a paradox, formal education can be seen as a hindrance to the development of certain highly talented and motivated people, for example within sports, arts, and…entrepreneurialism. The entrepreneurial university is however immune to such criticism. When these ideas are manifested in university practice, as they have been in several places across Europe, this becomes only all too clear.[13]

In Sweden, the ground was laid for implementing experiments with organizational forms such as the entrepreneurial university in 2010, when the Riksdag passed a government proposal to increase organizational autonomy for universities, in order to make them more flexible.[14] My

---

13. See, for instance, Martin Sperrer, Christina Müller, and Julia Soos, "The Concept of the Entrepreneurial University Applied to Universities of Technology in Austria: Already Reality or Visions of the Future?" *Technology Innovation Management Review* 6, no. 10 (2016): 37-44.

14. *En akademi i tiden – ökad frihet för universitet och högskolor*, Regeringens proposition 2009/10:149, https://www.regeringen.se/contentassets/07a972fdbfdd43789da5a5b03dbb6f4a/en-akademi-i-tiden---okad-frihet-for-universitet-och-hogskolor-prop.-200910149.

own university, Linnaeus University, founded that same year, seized the opportunity and almost immediately defined itself in line with these proposed entrepreneurial ideals. During 2012-2014 an interesting and thoroughly crafted project was carried through, setting the parameters for implementing this entrepreneurial ideology in all of its departments and activities. Being a new university, the burden of tradition was not there, and the motivation to experiment is therefore easy to understand. The project focused on two main issues: (1) to create a coherent rhetoric, or branding, and a "spirit" of entrepreneurialism at the university, and (2) to develop a toolbox for entrepreneurial learning. This second issue is interesting, because entrepreneurial learning is something rather different from institutionalizing a specific ideological overcoat on an established institution and something that can be, and is being, done in any university. More complicated is the practical implementation of an entrepreneurial identity across all faculties. Branding materials were produced, workshops were held, competence development courses were offered, and a huge re-organization of the university was implemented within the university, only four years after it was founded. "Normal" collegial and democratic decision-making structures were replaced by a steep hierarchical organization with executive power basically concentrated at only three levels: Prefect (institutional level), Dean (faculty level), and Vice-chancellor (university level). The motives for this change were the desire to increase speed in decision-making and "overcoming bureaucratic barriers," such as collegial boards and other organs threatening to slow things down.

The university brand took aim at which students were wanted and, once admitted, what they were to become. Policy was formulated on a distinctly personal level. The project website formulates the prospect of developed mind-sets in a number of indicative ways:

> The entrepreneurial university aims to take students from the role of a passive object to an action creative subject, or in pragmatic terms, to give students the skills to both generate ideas for change and to implement them. To achieve this, the project strives to work with involving methods, which better impact personal development and deeper layers of the personality.[15]

Now, universities have always had personal development as one of their core missions, and the idea that a person develops parts of his or her personality as a result of spending time there is by no means new. Humboldt's university ideals place personal development at its very core—students are to mature, and develop a refined spiritual and ethical character through diligent study and contemplation. As a result of this, the graduated young person becomes prepared to take part in civic life, with a firm moral compass and a sense of responsibility. This is, however, significantly different from an impact on "deeper layers of the personality" of the student considered within the realm of the entrepreneurial university.

> We believe that the entrepreneurial culture is developed by attitudes and competencies as a complement to the traditional literacy skills, which makes our students further attractive in the labor market. The entrepreneurial competence will in short, make a powerful tool to gain other knowledge and skills to increase the student's competitiveness on the market.[16]

---

15. Linnaeus University, "The Entrepreneurial University," https://lnu.se/en/meet-linnaeus-university/This-is-linnaeus-university/vision-and-basic-principles/the-entrepreneurial-university/.

16. Linnaeus University.

What is described here as "traditional" are "literacy skills" and these can of course be of various kinds which are all important to develop and cultivate.¹⁷ What is meant is perhaps that literacy skills are not primarily "traditional," but fundamental for anyone who is to develop an entrepreneurial mindset. To characterize literacy as traditional should be read as a rhetorical emphasis, situating the entrepreneurial university in a position of novelty, opposed even to the most fundamental skills taught by universities; properties such as those promoted by Wilhelm von Humboldt are not even necessary to mention. The goal is, explicitly, to increase the student's competitiveness on the market. The market can be interpreted as the labor market, but it just as well can be the economic market in a narrower sense, fostering the student to consider him or herself in terms of economically defined value, which is reasonable as that is the only real value governing an entrepreneur. But, am I not too simplistic here, too tendentious? Perhaps, but again, being entrepreneurial is not *per se* a problem—entrepreneurs are not by nature insidious proponents of egotism. Many of the most successful social movements and NGOs are driven by strong, entrepreneurial spirits, as for example Ingrid Newkirk of the People for the Ethical Treatment of Animals (PETA), Peter Benenson of Amnesty International, Robert Hunter of Greenpeace, and Nadezhda Tolokonnikova of the Pussy Riot punk-art collective. People such as these, however admirable they might be, tend to be in the minority and not the kind of entrepreneurs targeted by university rhetoric. Why? Because they tend to create disturbances; I will come back to this a

---

17. David Bawden, "Information and Digital Literacies: A Review of Concepts," *Journal of Documentation* 57 no. 2 (2001): 218-259.

bit later on. One can also be harsh, and claim that someone who personifies an "entrepreneurial spirit" does not need a university to tell her or him how to go about it, and those who do will probably never be true entrepreneurs.

So, who is this desired breed who will graduate from the university and how should they place themselves in society? One last quote from the Linnaeus University project helps clarify this:

> The mission is to create an entrepreneurial culture with students, teachers and researchers who are motivated and able to be active creators in a global knowledge economy characterized by high dynamics, high complexity and high uncertainty.[18]

Dynamics, complexity and uncertainty: the characteristics of the global knowledge economy. The idea is to create individuals who can manage that which is discussed more and more as the perhaps decisive property of contemporary social life: speed. Let us consider this for a while, leaving the specific case of the entrepreneurial university and looking instead at the contemporary university in a more general sense. What kind of culture is it actually fostering? The answer will in time prove to have a great deal of influence on the field of Library and Information Science.

## *Social Acceleration*

The logic is simple enough: as an entrepreneur you identify a situation or social need, assess it with regard to potential financial risk and gain, and at the same time assume that you are not alone in identifying the situation with similar

---

18. Linnaeus University.

intent. The choice is therefore to act or not to act, and the willingness to take the risk of being too quick is generally considered worth taking if potential revenue is high enough. Contemplation beyond that is really not an option. As this is the behavior that universities today, whether they choose a specific brand or not, want to implement in the "deeper layers of the personality" of the young people admitted to study, it is only reasonable that they seek out organizational forms that in themselves are manifestations of such speed and daring in decision-making. It is also no surprise that the pedagogical task of implementing these ideals needs to be directed at students, staff, and faculty alike. No salvation will come from a church run by non-believers. Universities, lecturers, and researchers do not however live in the idealistic vacuum envisioned by Humboldt or the *Magna Charta Universitatum*, but instead find themselves in the midst of the maelstrom of contemporary society: a society consumed by the idea of vehicularity and decisiveness. Speed permeates all sectors in society and it governs the way we communicate, as well as how and what we learn, or indeed need to learn.

Social acceleration has been one of the most prominent themes in critical social theory during the last few years and one of the most influential books on the subject is *Social Acceleration: A New Theory of Modernity* by German sociologist Hartmut Rosa. Rosa writes, as did Habermas and Honneth, within the Frankfurt School tradition. He is able to build on the conflictual thematics addressed by Honneth, suggesting that the dissolving of values attributed to traditional institutions and relations appears to have some common characteristics in that they are not, and this is interesting, really replaced by new structures of a similar kind. Instead, what is left is a kind of temporal flux, cultures of short-term projects (so prevalent in librarianship), insecurity in identities, and a sense that time is lacking and that this deficit is decisive in how we act and view ourselves and various societal processes around us. Rosa distinguishes three fundamental dimensions of social acceleration: (1) technical acceleration, (2) the acceleration of social change, and (3) the acceleration of the pace of life. Each of these three is intrinsically connected to the nothers, in a way that is sometimes on the verge of the paradoxical. One example is the way in which technological development has made it possible to save time in practical every-day issues—we do not have to line up in a bank anymore, but instead we do our bank businesses through our mobile devices—but we still experience an increased shortage of time in the balance between work and family life. Despite such observations, the three dimensions are distinguishable enough.

*Technical acceleration* is defined by Rosa as "the intentional, technical and above all technological (i.e. machine-based) acceleration of goal-directed processes."[19] The most obvious examples of this are processes related to communication, transportation, and the production of goods and services. This is in turn connected to the very essence of classical modernity in almost every conceivable area as seen in one of its most striking formulations, the *Manifesto de Futurismo*, published in 1909 by Filippo Tommaso Marinetti, which sparked new fire into aesthetic modernism.[20] The development of different modes of travel, from horse carriages to the Concorde in just a century, is telling. We find examples in librarianship as well,

---

19. Hartmut Rosa, *Social Acceleration: A New Theory of Modernity* (New York: Columbia University Press, 2015), 71.

20. Filippo Tommaso Marinetti, *The Founding and Manifesto of Futurism* (London: Art Press Books, 2016).

although they are less spectacular; think of the development of bibliographic practice from Konrad Gesner's pre-modern compilation of the *Biblioteca Universalis*, published in 1545 which was created by going through and writing down, manually, the stocks in numerous monastery libraries from Switzerland to Ireland, to punch-hole indexing cards in mid-20th century, to today's processes of automatic classification and Networked Knowledge Organization Systems. Yet another example is data processing, which can, as with any digitized processes, be accelerated to the speed of light, at least in theory. But, Rosa claims, data can be transferred but not generated at the speed of light; the pressure to accelerate increases as material interfaces have grown immensely as a direct result of the possibilities of digitization.[21] Within the dimension of technical acceleration are also the processes of organization, decision-making, administration, and control, for example, in public institutions and bureaucracies such as universities, as they too fall under the definition of goal-directed processes.

*The acceleration of social change* is closely linked with technical change as the former is much concerned with constructing tools to facilitate processes. Looking at universities, this becomes clear through not only the rationalization of administrative processes by means of digitization, but also by the choices of decision-making systems and organizational models. Rosa defines the acceleration of social change as "an increase of decay of action-oriented experiences and expectations and as a contraction of the time periods that determine the present

---

21. Rosa, *Social Acceleration*, 76.

of respective functional, value, and action spheres."[22] This applies to social and cultural institutions and practices alike. Politics are afflicted by an increasingly contracted present, with consequences for both historical consciousness and general attention spans—"past and future must be rewritten in the various areas of society at ever shorter intervals."[23] An example of this is the transformation of knowledge interests within the contemporary university, where the fostering of fundamental moral values and universal knowledge has been replaced by a politically induced mission to "solve" current societal challenges. Another interesting example can be seen in contemporary art and art education, with the coming of relational art and the so-called educational turn, where less energy is spent on the artefact or piece of art itself, but instead on collaborative, creative, and political processes surrounding its becoming.[24] This influences both consumption and production—audiences are increasingly interested in sketches and process discussions and the artist as such becomes, well, a kind of entrepreneur.

*The acceleration of the pace of life* is defined by Rosa as "an increase in episodes of action or experience per unit of time."[25] There are primarily two ways in which this particular dimension of acceleration shows itself in ordinary life: by doing things faster (for instance, family dining or end-term grading at work in order to get more time for family

---

22. *Ibid.*

23. Rosa, Social Acceleration, 77.

24. See, for instance, Nicholas Bourriaud, *Relational Aesthetics* (Paris: Les Presses du Réel, 2012) and Clair Bishop, *Artificial Hells: Participatory Art and the Politics of Spectatorship* (London: Verso, 2012).

25. Rosa, *Social Acceleration*, 78.

dining), or by reducing rest and empty time spaces between activities, sometimes to a point where several activities are being performed in parallel—multitasking. When this development reaches a breaking point, where a lack of time is experienced as such, there has been a condensation which may produce both stress and anxiety as well as a sense of not "keeping up" either at work or at home. The first victim of this particular form of acceleration is the work-life balance. Still, this is not new. Rosa concludes:

> Yet the fact that this experience of time has accompanied modern society in continually repeated waves since at least the eighteenth century does not prove that the pace of life in modernity has always been high, but rather strongly indicates that it constantly accelerates; it is a result of ever more scarce time resources. Strictly speaking, it says nothing at all about the 'absolute' tempo of life.[26]

This is an important remark, because it points to two things. First, the pace of life relates to an often-imaginary apprehension of what a healthy or normal life-pace should be. In doing so, references are often made to quite unachievable and sometimes abstract "ideal individuals" or situations such as indigenous cultural patterns representing something pre-modern or natural—or, for that matter, idealized working conditions in traditional libraries or the Humboldtian university. Second, such often-sentimental examples suggest that the contemporary pace is by definition a bad thing, leaving aside the fact that most people still generally tend to get a lot of things done properly. Looking at the specific version of the discussion on speed and acceleration within academia, this type of what we might call symbolic or, at

---

26. Rosa, *Social Acceleration*, 79.

worst, sentimental inertia is widespread and it takes on a number of characteristics.

## *Academia, Fast and Slow*

Speed and acceleration have become central in discussions about university development as well. As the European Higher Education Area defines universities as part of the general toolbox for solving current societal challenges and as strategic resources for innovation and economic growth, the need to be on the front line of the development that Rosa describes has been imposed on the sector due to external pressure. It is therefore no surprise to see a growing literature that challenge and even refuse the imposition of ideals that, at least superficially, seem to contradict the very idea of universities as institutions of learning. Nowhere perhaps is the "inversion of ideal" I earlier pointed to more clearly seen than in the conflict between those advocating a university for *Bildung* and self-improvement, and those putting the institution at the service of political fulfillment. The literature is vast and increasing, and stretches from pure moaning to initiated analyses. In order to make at least some sense of it, I will here focus on three dimensions of speed in academia that can, at least indirectly, all be related to the dimensions of Rosa: (1) organizational restructuring, (2) the well-being of scholars, and (3) the case for the humanities. Here, I will comment upon the first two, while the dimension concerning the humanities will be considered in more detail in chapter six, with specific reference to Library and Information Science.

The restructuring of universities that has gradually taken place during the last couple of decades differs within the EU and the US, although only slightly, due to national educational systems, bureaucratic traditions, and regional needs. The difference between the American corporate university and its European cousin, the entrepreneurial university, is an example of such differences in nuances and tradition. The development that has taken place, and we are still in the midst of it, has uniformity as one of its most distinctive characteristics. As universities adapt to the neoliberal narrative, issues concerning administration, organizational structures, and management need to be synchronized in a quite different way than that which we could see as the center of interest in the original Bologna Declaration. The chief ideal is rationalization of bureaucratic structures and creating conditions for fast decision-making. This has led to a number of consequences, one of which is the (felt) decrease of academic influence over directions taken, and an equal increase of the administrative professions within the university. In his much debated book *The Fall of the Faculty: The Rise of the All-Administrative University and Why It Matters*, Benjamin Ginsberg argues that universities have consistently worked towards a position where academic considerations have given way to managerial and administrative hegemony.[27] It becomes apparent in everything from the professionalization of administrative tasks, headhunting outside of academia for leadership positions, and the built-in inequality of the American tenure track system, something which does not (yet) exist within the European university system. The result is a focus on quick revenues, and rankings of everything from universities as such to the (academic) staff working in them. It also affects the production of knowledge itself. Ginsberg

---

27. Benjamin Ginsberg, *The Fall of the Faculty: The Rise of the All-Administrative University and Why It Matters* (Oxford: Oxford University Press, 2011).

addresses the situation in a largely anecdotal way, and at times he manages to capture some essential characteristics:

> From an administrative perspective, generally speaking, forms of knowledge that cannot profitably be sold to customers—be they students, corporations, the government, or private donors—should be scrapped in favor of investments in more financially promising areas of inquiry.[28]

Mark Edmundson formulates it in an even sharper way in an essay published in *The Hedgehog Review*:

> [A] new institutional culture is coming into being. Universities now team with people who must do what people who work in corporations do: be responsive to their superiors, direct their underlings, romance their Blackberries, subordinate their identities, refrain from making mistakes, keep a gimlet eye always on the bottom line. Organization men and women have come, and they are doing what they can—for an administrator must administer something—to influence the shape of the university.[29]

The impetus for critical inquiry is simply not there. These quotes remind me of what Paul Goodman writes in one of the appendices in the 2012 edition of his 1960 sociological classic *Growing Up Absurd*: "[m]y point is not that universities are worthless, nor that they should or cannot be free, but that one cannot seriously regard them as places of inquiry nor found the case of academic freedom on freedom of inquiry."[30] Putting these three quotes side by side pinpoints

---

28. Ginsberg, 168.

29. Mark Edmundson, "Under the Sign of Satan: William Blake in the Corporate University," *The Hedgehog Review* 14, no. 1 (2012): n.p.

30. Paul Goodman, (1960/2012) *Growing Up Absurd: Problems of Youth in the*

the problem of today's relation between, on the one hand, the claim to academic freedom threatened by administrative and economic pressure and, on the other, the alternative which far too often is put forward as the right to do research without being bothered by social realities and surroundings at all—the extreme version of the Humboldtian scholarly practice. Contemporary university hegemony solves this problem by its constant referral to "societal challenges" that need to be solved through "innovation."

This discourse of innovation limits the range of allowed or sanctioned research questions to those that fit the "acceleration of the pace of life" in Rosa's sense, and set up the premises for such inquiry through the competitive rhetoric I earlier brought to attention with the help of Filip Vostal.[31] What is interesting in Goodman's argument is that universities can only fulfill their democratic mission through a distinct relation between society and learning, one which must have the form of active social emancipation. For Goodman, this can be achieved through the creation of a distinct connection between knowledge and action. He argues that this connection can emerge in a defined development of the relation between objectivity and neutrality, where scientific inquiry should guard the former, but accept that the latter can never be achieved.[32] This is also the idea that informs the teaching practice of critical information literacy. In times such as ours, when objectivity and respect for facts are constantly undermined by growing political forces, Goodman's thoughts are still, almost sixty years after they

---

*Organized Society* (New York: New York Review Books, 1960/2012), 234.

31. Vostal, *Accelerating Academia*, 90-114.

32. Goodman, *Growing Up Absurd*, 246-247.

were first penned down, a crude reminder that there is a choice to be made in universities, by scholars. In order to internalize a social acceleration to which we are all subjected, individual scholars have a responsibility to choose what ideals should be followed—entrepreneurial drive for innovation or democratic and cultural emancipation.

Acceleration in academia becomes very real when discussed on the individual level, where scholars are pressed into conforming to the practices shaped by the ideals of the "all-administrative" structure of their university. But it does not stand uncontested. Inspired by Carl Honoré's bestselling book *In Praise of Slowness: Challenging the Cult of Speed*, a movement of slow scholarship has been steadily growing during the last decade.[33] A number of journals and online resources, such as *Times Higher Education*, *Forum: Qualitative Social Research/ Sozialforschung* and *The London School of Economics and Political Science Impact Blog*, have recurrently researched, analyzed, and debated the influence of increased speed, vehicularity, and fluidity in academic work and scholarly relations.

In this discussion some themes stand out, occurring regularly as specific points of concern relating to the structural and managerial issues I have touched upon thus far. I would like to address two of them: (1) the impact of quantification or "gamification" of research, and (2) the well-being of scholars and their relations to others.

I mentioned earlier that one of the reasons why universities, as opposed to libraries, have managed to adapt smoothly to

---

33. Carl Honoré, *In Praise of Slowness: Challenging the Cult of Speed* (New York: Harper Collins, 2005).

the neoliberal hegemony is that they can identify a crucial "selling-point" in contemporary society: knowledge. In order for this to become possible it has to be assigned a specific materiality, a product, within which knowledge can be packaged and delivered to customers. One such product is the scientific article. This is important as it explains a great deal about the ever-increasing demand on individual scholars to publish more and more, as well as the current transformation of the academic publishing industry. It is classic capitalist logic to rationalize in order to optimize output; scholars are forced to produce the greatest number of articles, in the shortest possible time. In order to achieve this, tools are created within the global scientific communication system to measure and assess scholars against each other. Competition becomes a key element in fostering productive professors. Scholarly online social media services such as ResearchGate and Academia.edu are built on principles of comparison and instant gratification as it is possible to follow and influence statistics of performance in terms of actual output, citations, and personal networks. Even institutional repositories such as DiVA, the one most commonly used by Swedish universities, include statistics related to the number of downloads and "reads" of individual posts or full-text documents. As performance measurements within these services and platforms are combined with a growing number of general performance indicators, Peter Dahler-Larsen argues that they achieve an actual constitutive effect:

> [t]his concept suggests that our practices are formed, shaped and reconstituted in the light of indicators which in fact define that which they claim to measure. One of the constitutive

effects of indicators is to create more competitive relationships between all those whose scores are compared.[34]

As participation on platforms such as ResearchGate is voluntary, the harm and, of course, the benefit that they create is limited. It becomes another matter when bibliometric indicators and competitive inducements are used by departments to grant tenure, give promotions, set wages, and allocate research time for individual scholars. In most countries today, this is where we are at, resulting in client organization versions of Clark Kerr's knowledge factories. A culture of self-promotion or self-entrepreneurialism is fostered in which researchers are not just supposed to publish at increasing rates, but also to promote themselves on the basis of statistics indicating their productive capacity. Jeffrey Williams writes about this in an article in the *Chronicle of Higher Education*, calling it "the rise of the promotional intellectual"—a neoliberal version of the more immediately recognizable public intellectual.[35] However, as some commentators on academic vehicularity have pointed out, not all aspects of speed in general or the use of social media in particular, need to be detrimental. There is also an alternative narrative, where indicators can be both liberating and emancipating through increased visibility of important research, can function as motivation for young researchers to achieve peer recognition, and can help build networks as

---

34. Peter Dahler-Larsen, "The New Configuration of Metrics, Rules, and Guidelines Creates a Disturbing Ambiguity in Academia," *LSE Impact Blog*, July 13, 2017.

35. Jeffrey J. Williams, "The Rise of the Promotional Intellectual," *Chronicle of Higher Education*, August 5, 2018.

well as influence the dissemination of research results to the general public.[36]

On a structural and organizational level, it is well established that the contemporary university fosters the fundamental neoliberal logic of increased speed in production of scientific and teaching output, and that the use of quantitative indicators is prevalent in controlling and directing research in a politically desired way. If we assume, which is reasonable to do, that most professors and teachers enter academia with a different conception of what it means to do research and teach, we find an important conflict. If, as has been suggested here, work is instrumentalized and guided by shortsighted "knowledge needs" formulated in a managerial relation to the surrounding society and industry, people should feel very badly in universities. Studies on this subject do, however, provide a relatively nuanced picture of the experience of time in universities. There seems to be a general agreement that work speed is increasing, and that this leads primarily to a lack of three things: time to think, sufficient time to take breaks between an ever-increasing number of daily tasks, and time to engage in meaningful conversations with, for instance, students. Filip Vostal conducted an interview study with twenty Russell Group scholars in the UK and found that (1) acceleration and high speed in daily work is not experienced only as pathological, nor is it perceived as health-threatening; still, there is a distinct sense of running on a "treadmill" faster and faster, and (2) academics across disciplines, contrary to much of the research in this field, seem to actually enjoy positive

---

36. Björn Hammarfelt, Sarah de Rijcke, and Alexander D. Rushforth, "Quantified Academic Selves: The Gamification of Research through Social Networking Services," *Information Research* 21 no. 2 (2016), Paper SM1.

subjective experiences of speed, not least if they correspond with the pace of development in the social sectors relevant for consumers of the completed research.[37] It can, probably with good reason, be objected that the informants in Vostal's study are perhaps not the most representative group in academia. All are senior scholars in UK prestige universities, who are most certainly enjoying exactly the "time to think" and ability to interact with students that much of the literature points to as being problematic in other settings. Still, the assumption that academics on a general level are simply victims of structural preconditions is likely to be false.

What perhaps should be at the center of the discussion is another question: what acceleration in academia does to the ability to pursue critical analyses that do not necessarily conform with the prioritized learning and knowledge outcomes desired by the university. The ability to apply critical perspectives and to make room to create alternative models and constructs is not encouraged by entrepreneurial universities, nor is it emphasized in strategic research policy, whether on European or national levels. This particular problem does indeed recur as a pressing one in the discussion on accelerating academia. Maggie O'Neill proposes that scholars, as intellectuals, "need to think through the structures of feeling that have emerged across the sector and to work on containing anxiety in the system and indeed consider the potential of slow radicalism, as a counter approach to the fast university and its impact on work, time and well-being."[38] This is seconded by Maggie Berg and Barbara Seeber in their

---

37. Vostal, *Accelerating Academia*, 115-141.

38. Maggie O'Neill, "The Slow University: Work, Time and Well-Being," *Forum: Qualitative Social Research / Sozialforschung* 15, no. 3 (2014), Art. 14.

rewardingly personal account *The Slow Professor: Challenging the Culture of Speed in the Academy*, in which they focus on the situation of scholars in the humanities—they are both professors of English. In "The Slow Professor Manifesto" they state that "[w]e are slow professors. We believe that adopting the principles of Slow into our professional practice is an effective way to alleviate work stress, preserve humanistic education and resist the corporate university."[39] They wish, as does Vostal, to challenge not only the ideology and practical demands of current university policy, but also the victimizing character of the discussion, and instead hail the possibility of finding a way around alienation and knowledge consumerism: "[R]esistance is alive and well. We envisage Slow Professors acting purposefully, cultivating emotional and intellectual resilience. By taking the time for reflection and dialogue, the Slow Professor takes back the intellectual life of the university."[40]

Berg and Seeber are right to approach the neoliberal university with this positive, normative stance. The higher education sector has, through its focus on contributing to economic growth by competitive practices and entrepreneurial ideals, and despite the apparent discomfort of many of its scholars, become the very opposite of the free educational institution of the *Magna Charta Universitatum*. It has instead turned in to an accomplice of a political development that is now leading us all in a direction that opposes the very fundamentals of liberal democracy. What

---

39. Maggie Berg and Barbara K. Seeber, *The Slow Professor: Challenging the Culture of Speed in the Academy* (Toronto: University of Toronto Press, 2016), ix.

40. Berg and Seeber, x.

we see is a systematic and deliberate social deconstruction where universities try to remain "relevant" by fostering a non-critical position towards everything from educational and research policy to management forms implemented to satisfy the misapprehension that quality is equal to quantitative performance measurement—be that through bibliometric indicators, productivity measures, or uncritical use of administrative technology. The pace of life in this world of instrumental learning and commodified research output is such that it does not promote critical thinking, despite the fact that critical thinking is exactly that is needed at this point in our common political history.

The next question is where all this puts Library and Information Science. There is no doubt that embedded rhetorical concepts such as "information society" and "knowledge society" have benefited the discipline for decades and made it possible for its scholars to fit well into the present ideological hegemony, both intellectually and organizationally. How this is being done is the focus of the next chapter. Underneath it all lies the question: what does all this mean for the education of librarians? After all, the profession of librarianship is at the heart of the discipline's striving for legitimacy although, as I noted at the beginning, not everybody would agree with such a claim. The reason for this is that libraries and librarians are a bit uncomfortable in the ethically lacking social environment of neoliberalism. At the end of the day, that is a good thing.

## Chapter 4

### THE OPEN CORE OF LIBRARY AND INFORMATION SCIENCE

One of the main characteristics of any profession is the presence of an intellectual platform provided by education and research. Librarianship, of course, is no exception. There is, however, no one rule about what the relationship between practice and theory is supposed to look like. On the one hand there is a need for evidence-based practice, and on the other hand there is an academic drive for independent research concerning the development of theory. Neither of these, some would argue, are particularly important for the advancement of Library and Information Science or, as a consequence, professional librarianship. Evidence-based practice is a child of contemporary managerial ideals craving unambiguous results and best practice examples: "this works" is the mantra. If this is formulated by researchers rather than practitioners (or by a combination of the two), evidence is strong. The advantage of evidence-based practice is that results and "evidence" tend to be of the sort that can be quickly implemented and put into place in new settings and local environments without further ado. This is in line with the kind of knowledge promoted by entrepreneurial universities and the political demands for applicability, accountability, and speedy decision-making in organizations. It does not, however, cover the needs of the profession, nor the depth and breadth of the discipline. Instead, in a narrow New Public Management environment, which is today as omnipresent in librarianship as it is in universities, accounts are now coming in of almost a kind of guerilla warfare against managerial pressure, with initiatives to create a true intellectual platform within practice, one that is scientific as well as moral. Examples are given in Karen Nicholson and Maura Seale's anthology *The Politics of Theory and the Practice of Critical Librarianship*, where everything is discussed from justice-oriented "indigenization" agendas in literacy practice to the use of philosophical reading groups for academic librarians to reflect on their own daily work.[1] The meaning of having an intellectual platform in the form of a research base for professional librarianship clearly extends the claims for evidence-based librarianship, as the role of Library and Information Science education and research stretches far beyond providing the means for such practices. These may seem like trivial remarks, but they are still worth expressing, as Library and Information Science as an academic discipline is by no means easy to grasp. In librarianship, questions are frequently raised about what the discipline is actually about, how it connects to the profession, and how it is relevant to social and technological development. There are in many cases good reason for this bewilderment. The discipline does indeed have an internal logic which may seem arcane to those outside of it and, unfortunately, also to many on the inside of it.

In this chapter, I will discuss Library and Information Science from two perspectives: epistemological and

---

1. Karen P. Nicholson and Maura Seale, eds., *The Politics of Theory and the Practice of Critical Librarianship* (Sacramento, CA: Library Juice Press, 2018).

organizational. This will be done by looking at relatively general descriptions and discussions with only limited reference to library practice. This particular relationship will instead be discussed separately in the next chapter, focusing on the development of the iSchool movement. In that chapter, I will take a theoretical look at the current institutional and organizational developments within the discipline, in an attempt to understand this "movement" as part of the transformation of library education with the goal of aligning with university ideals as previously discussed. The discipline of Library and Information Science has for several decades been subjected to debate concerning its epistemological character and paradigmatic development. In the early 1990s this was addressed through the development of the Conceptions of Library and Information Science (CoLIS) conference series, still considered one of the most prominent in the discipline.[2] My aim here is to capture some of the essential findings in today's discussion in order to draw conclusions about their implications for librarianship. As material conditions tend to influence how we think, it is reasonable to assume that new forms of disciplinary organization and new positions in higher education institutions also affect the content of the discipline. But, before we get into that particular discussion,

---

2. Proceedings of the first two CoLIS conferences were published as: Pertti Vakkari and Blaise Cronin, eds., *Conceptions of Library and Information Science: Historical, Empirical and Theoretical perspectives: Proceedings of the International Conference Held for the Celebration of the 20th Anniversary of the Department of Information Studies, University of Tampere, Finland, 26-28 August 1991* (London: Taylor Graham, 1992) and Peter Ingwersen and Niels Ole Pors, eds., *Information Science: Integration in Perspective: Proceedings of the Second International Conference on Conceptions of Library and Information Science, October 13-16, 1996, Copenhagen, Denmark* (Copenhagen: The Royal School of Librarianship, 1996)..

let us have a look at epistemology—what kind of knowledge is actually generated through the study of Library and Information Science, and about what?

## *Library and Information Science—An Epistemological Enigma?*

In a famous article from the turn of the latest century, Birger Hjørland subjects the knowledge claims of Library and Information Science to a thorough analysis. "The most critical question for developing a corpus of knowledge in librarianship, documentation, and information science, has been," he states, "the problem of subject knowledge: how to develop *general* knowledge, which does not dissolve into subject knowledge."[3] Ways of addressing this problem have been focused on information technologies, psychological models, and, in Hjørland's own case, domain analysis. There are mainly two problems at play here: (1) the status as a "pure" or at least coherent science, directed towards theory generation, and (2) dependency on factors external to academia, such as the intellectual needs of library institutions and general social development. In the former, development is more or less linear, with corroboration or refutation of experimental and empirical findings as the basis for new knowledge claims. In the latter, problems are (at least in part) defined by others than researchers, for instance from within professional practice, resulting in applied research. The question is if these two perspectives cannot be combined, and instead of being defined as conflictual, be considered

---

3. Birger Hjørland, "Library and Information Science: Practice, Theory, and Philosophical Basis," *Information Processing and Management* 36 (2000): 510-531. Italics in original.

as complementary. Library and Information Science shares this fundamental problem with many other disciplines, most notably medicine, which is a good example of how research combines general knowledge claims and practice. For example, specific branches of medicine such as etiology or research concerning the relation between environment, lifestyle choices, and health—this is general knowledge in the service of increased diagnostic accuracy and refined therapies at local hospitals. Law is another example with general, scientifically relevant problems tied closely to legislative practice and daily work in courtrooms and industry. It is, however, here that we also see the epistemological conundrum, if indeed one exists.

Hjørland claims that "[i]t is a well-known fact that LIS lacks good theories."[4] Now this may be true in a narrow sense, but in the end it all comes down to what theory is supposed to be—and do. In a discipline such as Library and Information Science, as in medicine or law, the role of theory should be thought of as something that helps to enhance a general understanding of specific practices which have been defined and redefined over a long period of time, with certain elements remaining more or less consistent while others change. One of the factors contributing to such a redefinition is new theoretical knowledge. This follows the argument I made in chapter one, concerning an ongoing tension between tradition and innovation in library practice. Hjørland's problem is one shared by many during the relatively short history of Library and Information Science. I claim that there is no lack of "good theory" in Library and Information Science, and there was not when Hjørland published his article, either. Theory development has always had a character

---

4. Hjørland, 518.

seen as problematic by those seeking refuge in traditional, positivistic, or "modern" theory development. Instead, we must look at it in direct relation to established professional and societal practices. When we do that, we instead find a discipline with a quite healthy and relevant theory development, albeit not one without problems of ambiguity.

A few years before Hjørland's article appeared, Michael Buckland made a similar kind of argument concerning the historically significant problem of the relation between the academic discipline and the practice of librarianship.[5] However, the way in which he addresses the issue is different from Hjørland's. Instead of relating the discipline to ideal theory development and the quest for one comprehensive problem at its center, Buckland targets the relation between professional stability, technological innovation, and the lack of scholarly communication. He points to several decisive factors. First, Library and Information Science in the US was formed around the Graduate Library School at the University of Chicago. The Carnegie Corporation founded it with the goal of having it become for librarianship what Harvard Law School and Johns Hopkins Medical School had become in their respective fields. This ambition resulted in a formulation of a sociological paradigm distancing the development of Library and Information Science as well as librarianship from the more visionary theorizing taking place within the European documentation movement. These developments subsequently created a simultaneous consolidation, placing Library and Information Science firmly at the intersection between social sciences and humanities, paired with

---

5. Michael Buckland, "Documentation, Information Science, and Library Science in the USA". *Information Processing and Management* 32, no. 1 (1996): 63-76.

an increased interest in design and technology within library services as formulated through the activities of La Fédération d'Information et de Documentation (FID) and its predecessors. As this latter development was created mainly by people outside of librarianship, an Information Science side of the discipline emerged, leading to an unfortunate but persistent division between "librarians" and "technologists" visible on both sides of the Atlantic. This has been a central concern of many prominent academics and practitioners within the field, most notably perhaps Jesse Hauk Shera.[6] I have elsewhere shown that this division persisted in various forms well into, and past, the turn of the century.[7] Buckland ends his study by stating that:

> [t]he temporary de-emphasis of design and technology contributed to a prolonged failure of identity and direction in the academic departments of library and information studies.... Absent a central concern with design and technique, a coherent vision for research and for university-based professional education is also absent.[8]

To have this kind of conflict in a discipline such as Library and Information Science is not unusual or even unproductive.

---

6. H. Curtis Wright, *Jesse Shera, Librarianship, and Information Science* (Sacramento, CA: Library Juice Press, 2013), 39-58.

7. Joacim Hansson, "The Social Legitimacy of Library and Information Science: Reconsidering the institutional paradigm" in *Aware and Responsible: Papers of the Nordic-International Colloquium on Social and Cultural Wwareness and Responsibility in Library, Information and Documentation Studies (SCARLID)*, ed. W. Boyd Rayward (Lanham, MD: Scarecrow Press, 2004), 49-69.

8. Buckland, "Documentation, Information Science, and Library Science in the USA," 74.

But it does challenge our views on how to understand and make use of the scholarly platform for librarianship. It is important that we see Library and Information Science as just that, a scholarly platform which not only deals with technique and increased systems performance but also with a more normative side of the profession. Thus, epistemological development is of great concern and the fact that there is little consensus on how to characterize the discipline is in itself telling. For instance, the interest in "information behavior" in people's daily lives or in various professional settings, does not just search for the fulfillment of theoretical conclusions based on definitions of information combined with models drawn primarily from cognitive sciences. It furthers our understanding of the development of search algorithms and psychological manipulation through social media and provides a deeper sense of the vulnerability of humans when trying to make sense of the world through the use of information. It also matters how the role of institutions such as libraries, museums, and archives should be defined and none of them are done justice by placing technological development and trends at the center of interest. Looking at the discipline today we see that this is no longer the case, either in the choice of research focus or in methodology.

## *Contemporary Perspectives*

One of the most comprehensive accounts of contemporary perspectives or paradigms within Library and Information Science is the French treatise *La science de l'information: origines, théories et paradigmes* by Fidelia Ibekwe-SanJuan.[9]

---

9. Fidelia Ibekwe-SanJuan, *La science de l'information: origines, théories et paradigmes* (Paris: Lavoisier, 2012).

She identifies five main epistemological streams, running side by side in Library and Information Science today:

- *Rationalism and positivism*, particularly in classification and the search for standards in the organization of knowledge,
- *Empiricism*, particularly visible in research on bibliometrics and scientific communication,
- *Cognitivism*, traditionally seen in user studies,
- *Social constructivism*, as seen in, for instance, domain analysis and attempts to transgress the gap between individual and collective levels of analysis, and
- *Pragmatism*, particularly in parts of the discipline relating to social linguistics.

For anyone even remotely knowledgeable about the theory of Library and Information Science, these paradigms come as no surprise—nor are they intended to. They have all been widely covered in the literature of the discipline. What is emphasized and well formulated by Ibekwe-SanJuan is how all of them live parallel lives. Some, and she suggests pragmatism as a good example, may be seen as permeating all the others, providing a bedrock upon which various paradigmatical appearances may be constructed and situated. The paradigms of Library and Information Science do not come in any successive order. Instead, they tend to dominate specific sub-areas of the discipline, thus proving that the question of what is the actual object of study in Library and Information Science is, in some sense, put wrongly. There are certain concepts which all of these paradigms and subfields circle around, such as "information," "information practices," and "document," "documentation," or "documentation practices." More recently, we can also add "data" and in some cases "big data." I will not discuss these concepts further at this point, but instead will return to them in the final chapter of this book, as the relation between them is at the very core of developing a progressive agenda for future research in the field.

For now, it is sufficient that we find ourselves in a position where it is reasonable to assume that discussing the epistemological character of Library and Information Science is something which may not be easily done if we stick to traditional views on disciplinary or theoretical development, or reject the influence of situational factors such as social and technological development or professional practice. As research problems change over time at increasing speed, we should perhaps instead turn to analyze the legitimacy of specific problems in relation to normative positions in the use and institutionalization of information and documentation as the basis for a scholarly discipline. Defying the idea of universalism in terms of time and geography in information practices as well in the organization of documents and knowledge is (still) an interesting thought, not least now as the issue of universalism is under such strain. The impact of national and regional educational systems, political structures, varieties of social strata, and technological access should not be underestimated. This is seen also in the relation between the epistemological and the organizational level since, as Jan Nolin and Fredrik Åström suggest in an influential article published in the *Journal of Documentation:* "LIS departments will…to a large extent be shaped by local factors."[10]

---

10. Jan Nolin and Fredrik Åström, "Turning Weakness into Strength: Strategies for Future LIS," *Journal of Documentation* 66, no. 1 (2010): 10.

Nolin and Åström make a strong argument that Library and Information Science is characterized by a tension between convergence and divergence in a way that is deemed problematic in normal science, which strives to avoid anomalies and create mono-disciplinary entities with successive paradigmatic shifts. However, if seen as a "post-normal" science, this conflict can be turned into a sign of strength, as it opens up the possibility of studying a connected variety of problems from multi-angular perspectives. The perhaps most distressing problem that a discipline such as Library and Information Science has to confront is that of "reputational autonomy," which directly affects the material prerequisites for development in local and national settings. Reputational autonomy relates to the ability to describe, and argue for, a unique field of inquiry within a discipline. In a field so characterized by epistemological divergence as is Library and Information Science, one consequence may be difficulties in attracting funding in competition with other, less divergent fields. Nolin and Åström provide the example of the Finnish and Swedish national research councils, whose research applications tend to be assessed in review groups with no, or very few, scholars with insight into the discipline. It is sometimes even hard to argue for a true case of trans-disciplinarity as the paradigms shown by Ibekwe-SanJuan tend to run in parallel with very limited communication between them. Nolin and Åström describe certain attempts to come to terms with such problems, defining them as "turns," where one of the more constructive efforts may be Peter Ingwersen and Kalervo Järvelin's suggestion to bring together information retrieval research with the information-seeking subfield, through the formulation of an "extended cognitive viewpoint."[11] However, no initiative in Library and Information Science (Nolin and Åström mention no less than eleven "turns") solves the problem of reputational autonomy. Not at least for as long as research councils and universities prioritize traditional criteria for funding distribution. This may, however, now be beginning to be change. While it still tends to be difficult for Library and Information Science researchers to attract funding via the general annual calls put out by national research agencies, an increased number of policies concerning more specialized, problem-oriented calls are now gaining ground.

One such example, which is by no means unique, was started in the spring of 2018 by the Swedish Research Council; it focuses on digitization as a means of providing access to cultural heritage collections. The purpose statement of the call is formulated as follows:

> The focus of this grant aims to promote digitisation of and better accessibility to cultural heritage collections, primarily within humanities and social sciences, but also within other scientific fields of great value to research. The Swedish Research Council rewards research of the highest scientific quality in national competition.[12]

This is a call prompted by an attempt to merge a social need with technical availability in a way which suits collaboration not only between disciplines or, in the case

---

11. Peter Ingwersen and Kalervo Järvelin, *The Turn: Integration of Information Seeking and Retrieval in Context* (Dordrecht: Springer, 2005).

12. *Research Project Grant for Digitisation and Accessibility of Cultural Heritage Collections*. Swedish Research Council, 2018, https://vr.se/english/calls-and-decisions/calls/calls/2018-06-05-research-project-grant-for-digitisation-and-accessibility-of-cultural-heritage-collections.html.

of Library and Information Science, between parts of post-normal disciplines, but also with institutional agents outside of academia. A few things are worth noting in this call: (1) the research council is usually devoted to supporting basic research; here, accessibility to cultural heritage is treated as interesting in itself and as a social need that can be met through available technology, (2) research efforts are defined as part of what we usually call digital humanities, which has a defined primary knowledge interest in the humanities and the social sciences, and (3) what is rewarded is the "highest scientific quality," which in this collaborative and practice-oriented field means playing down the tension between basic and applied research in order to solve a social challenge or need—here, increased and equal access to cultural heritage. This kind of approach has always been considered a problem by those advocating for a strong convergence of the discipline, that is a paradigmatical consolidation in accordance with "normal" science. In the empirical environment in which Library and Information Science scholars operate and theorize, this is of course a minor problem and today, it is my impression at least, the question of epistemological convergence is less and less emphasized. Perhaps the world around us is starting to catch up, or perhaps there are other reasons. Perhaps it turns out that Library and Information Science is well suited to meet the ambition of the neoliberal university in that its divergent character and its openness fit the kind of knowledge promoted and that the entrepreneurial university craves so much in order to legitimize the value of its brand. Who defines the research problems in each call is therefore of less importance. With the risk of over-dramatizing the significance of this call, it is interesting as an example of a way of formulating research needs that fit disciplines like

Library and Information Science, museology, or archival science well. Do calls like this increase the ability of Library and Information Science to attract funding? In this case and at the time this is written, it is something which remains to be seen. But, is it possible to understand consequences in more general terms, when it comes to institutional development and the relation to defined social sectors and professional practices, as in libraries or the GLAM sector as a whole?

Nolin and Åström address this question in light of the conflictual tendencies between epistemological and organizational conditions in the field. It is interesting, not least in relation to the development of the iSchool movement now sweeping across the globe. Let me quote how they sum up the problem:

> Institutional and epistemological integration are two very different strategies. In the former case, the identity of LIS is weakened every time a department is converted into an i-school, although…the i-schools at Drexel and The University of Washington often are mentioned as examples of LIS success stories. With epistemological integration there is an attempt to find a traditional disciplinary core that can serve as a resource in the context of the competition problem. There is also an obvious risk with that kind of movement, since it may serve to streamline what is actually a very heterogeneous research field and thereby exclude researchers. These may instead gravitate toward other disciplines.[13]

In other words, it's quite a mess, but what character that mess takes depends among other things on the fundamental academic culture of the departments in question. Nolin and Åström suggest that strength can be gained from a combination of epistemological convergence (concentration on problems

---

13. Nolin and Åström, "Turning Weakness into Strength," 16.

and knowledge interests) and divergence in organizational settings (flexible, transdisciplinary departments), thus leading to a "strong identity" that is "connected to a wide range of academic disciplines."[14] The conflict between attempts for epistemological convergence in a situation of organizational divergence tend to be treated differently depending on the surrounding academic environment. It matters where on the science-humanities scale the discipline is placed, on either level. It matters in everything from how problems are addressed and what methodologies are chosen, to how results are presented and communicated. And, it must be added, it matters in relation to social, technological, and political development—the idea of equal access to a common cultural heritage through digital representation is an example of that. The call from the Swedish Research Council is nothing other than an implementation of a political will.

So where do Library and Information Science departments belong? Jeannie Borup Larsen did a survey for a unique gathering of European Library and Information Science scholars which took place in Copenhagen in 2005 concluding that, at that point in time, thirty-five percent of the European departments were situated as parts of cross-disciplinary institutions or faculties in the humanities and social science.[15] The rest were scattered over other kinds of departments, with only four percent connected to computer science and six percent being autonomous LIS schools. These figures came

---

14. Nolin and Åström, 16.

15. Jeannie Borup Larsen, "A Survey of Library and Information Schools in Europe," in *European Curriculum Reflections on Library and Information Science Education*, eds. Leif Kajberg and Leif Lorring (Copenhagen: Royal School of Library and Information Science, 2005), 232-241.

out before the expansion of the iSchools Organization, but concern for the discipline's academic "home" is still valid. For example, when the Royal School of Library and Information Science, one of the few European standing members of the iSchools Organization's top tier, the iCaucus, was transferred from its previous autonomous status to becoming an academic department at the University of Copenhagen in 2013, the school was placed within the Faculty of Humanities under the name Department of Information Studies. In Sweden, three out of five Library and Information Science departments are placed within cultural studies institutions, one is in a sociology department, and one is a semi-autonomous school.[16] The question of institutional placement is interesting and directly relates to the epistemological claims that various proponents have made over several decades. A discipline which does not adhere to the general sentiment of its academic affiliation is surely bound to fail—both in formulating a sufficiently convergent epistemological position and, on the more material side of life, in attracting sufficient funding and public interest that is needed to flourish and develop. From a European perspective, Library and Information Science is a discipline at the intersection between social sciences and the humanities.

In a conceptual piece with the somewhat challenging title "What Kind of Science *Can* Information Science Be?", Michael Buckland addresses the issue from yet another angle, down-playing the convergence/divergence brain-teaser and instead arguing that as a discipline, Library and Information Science should be aware of the prerequisites of

---

16. Joacim Hansson, Åse Hedemark, Ulrika Kjellman, Jenny Lindberg, Jan Nolin, Olof Sundin, and Per Wisselgren, *Profession, utbildning forskning: biblioteks- och informationsvetenskap för en stärkt bibliotekarieprofession* (Stockholm: Kungliga Biblioteket, 2018).

paradigmatical prominence and relations.[17] Various subfields simply have different degrees of scientific claims. He shows that it is somewhat paradoxical that information retrieval and bibliometrics emerged in the 1950s and 1960s respectively as being, on the one hand, the most "scientific" and quantitative subfields and, on the other hand, extremely pragmatic and design-oriented. In the same manner, information-seeking research or user studies can be criticized for building, also in its more cognitivistic appearances, on a fundamentally behavioristic model. Buckland points out the lack of recognition of the well-established fact that knowledge is incremental and that the negligence of this decreases the value of much of the information-seeking research being done. He blames this problem partly on the dependency on a concept of information which has never been sufficiently worked through and operationalized within the field, something which becomes more acute the further away from a critical social science and a culturally-based point of departure that we get. Instead, he suggests a shift (a turn?) towards a more document-oriented view of the material and social processes that are at the center of interest for the divergent Library and Information Science discipline. If the notion of information as a fundamental of the discipline is connected to knowledge and learning on an epistemological level, and connected to the material production, dissemination, and use of documents, it will lead to certain consequences. Buckland outlines four:

> First, there is a separation from the essentially knowledge-free zones occupied by computer science, the physics of

---

17. Michael Buckland, "What Kind of Science *Can* Information Science Be?" *Journal of the American Society for Information Science and Technology* 63, no. 1 (2012): 1-7.

information, and information technology. Second, any notion of information studies involving what and how we know can only be a cultural inquiry. Third, useful formal and quantitative tools depend on significant simplifying compromises needed to diminish the subjective and cultural qualities of the field. Finally, accepting the cultural context of information science should lead to a more realistic and more effective contribution to our document-pervaded society.[18]

I find Buckland's conclusions valid, and I maintain that there is nothing that should be fixed here. There is no ideal or definitive way in which to organize Library and Information Science on an epistemological level. Instead, we recognize how these different sides of the discipline fertilize each other in the pursuit of knowledge. It doesn't look this way because second-rate researchers inhabit a discipline with a lack of relevant theoretical and methodological development. Instead one must look at the discipline's place in the world and doing so, it now seems reasonable to take the discipline into a more document-focused direction. It develops the way it does because it relates to a defined social sector, whether formulated as a library sector or as an iField, which (1) is home to a number of relevant questions, from practical skill development (cataloging is a good traditional example) to more complex theoretical analyses within the humanities or social sciences, and (2) has developed significantly over the last couple of decades in order to meet this social complexity. What Buckland points to is that this development has taken place mainly on the level of skills development, primarily in information and communication technology. This is, however, nothing new—librarians have over the years struggled with the emergence of everything from paperbacks and television

---

18. Buckland, "What Kind of Science *Can* Information Science Be?" 6.

to movies and computerized catalogs with sound skepticism and have incorporated innovations in documentation as parts of basic services in due time. What has perhaps not changed in the same profound way is the deeper problems that this development is meant to address—whether on individual/cognitive or collective levels.

Library and Information Science is a scholarly discipline with an open core. It is placed at the cross-road between instrumental, technically-defined skill and tool development (Buckland's "knowledge-free zones") and more complex social-humanistic knowledge interests. Which of these achieve hegemonic status depends to a large degree on the higher educational environment of the day. In the case of our present particular discipline, it also depends on the ideals governing the professional sector it is designed to meet the needs and trends of. Although "library schools" have persisted to a perhaps surprisingly high degree, and with great success at that, they have been challenged at least since the late 1970s when librarians started taking about themselves as information professionals. IFLA serves as an umbrella organization for associations representing both. The way in which the information paradigm ties the discipline to the private information industry has changed what is perceived as useful knowledge and has also defined a new kind of obsolete. This is an important part of the process of including the public sphere in the competitive environment that up until quite recently has been limited to the private sector. Perhaps a bit over-dramatically, this can be described as a battle of fundamental concepts within the discipline. On the one hand, there are those who embrace information as the key element in the new social economy, relating the discipline to the commercial sector where libraries and professional librarianship are often seen, if not as a liability, at least as something that has to be re-furnished to fit into a new discourse. On the other hand, there are those who prioritize documents or documentation in a more scholarly approach. It should be quite safe to say that it is the former that has the upper hand at the moment and will continue to have it for the foreseeable future. The needs of the user (customer) and increased pressure from universities to address "societal challenges" re-writes the legitimacy of the discipline. This bears consequences on a material level in terms of departmental structure and relations to other disciplines. Over the last decade there has been a movement towards broadened organizational forms, concurrent with demands to reduce the gap between industry and higher education. The inclusion of a more innovation-oriented focus in universities has, definitely in Europe, led to a need to revise such things as the relationship between Library and Information Science and computer science. In the US, integration between industry and academic disciplines is something which is embedded in the very DNA of higher education; in Europe not so much and not in the same way. It has been prominent in technological disciplines such as computer science, but is scarcer in the social sciences and the humanities. Through the development of major political initiatives to develop cross-disciplinary research agendas by means of constructs such as digital humanities, this is currently changing. Nowhere in Library and Information Science is this transformation seen more clearly than at the iConference, the annual social gathering of the iSchools Organization. The iConference is in many ways just another conference, ripe with the usual academic cult rituals and invisible power strata, albeit with a significantly more visible presence from the commercial information industry than is usually found on other similar occasions within the discipline. It is the window into the timeliness of the discipline. The bigger and more serious questions lurking in the dark, surprisingly seldom asked, is what kind of creature the iSchools Organization actually is and what effect does it have on Library and Information Science education and research, which have traditionally been legitimized through a distinct connection to professional librarianship. Let us consider these questions—it is now time to enter the world of iSchools.

## Chapter 5

### THE iSCHOOL MOVEMENT—AN ANSWER TO WHICH QUESTION?

Perhaps the most interesting development for Library and Information Science during the last decade is the expansion of the iSchools Organization, or the iSchool "movement" as some prefer to call it. There are, at the time of this writing, eighty-two iSchools worldwide. Thirty-eight of these are situated in North America, twenty-eight in Europe (including Israel), and sixteen in the Asian/Pacific region. In addition to these regular member schools, there are seven "associated members." iSchool member departments by no means constitute a majority of all those which teach Library and Information Science, but they do manage to attract a lot of attention. Therefore, they are interesting. In this chapter, I will contemplate what this development means for Library and Information Science both in terms of its knowledge claims and its relationship to librarianship, and for the discipline's position in the spectrum of scholarly disciplines.

iSchools are interesting both as a movement and as the more concrete iSchools Organization. To label something as a movement is quite different from being an organization. A movement is generally seen as something which preambles the founding of a formal organization. In the case of iSchools, however, it is not quite certain which came first; the gradual formation of the iCaucus and the expanded iSchools Organization are talked about mainly as a movement in relation to its international expansion, which started when the organization as such was already in place. So, it matters, and the idea of a movement is interesting. A social (or educational) movement is an inclusive phenomenon which attracts members or advocacy by means of a strong mission or ethos. It may or may not be tied to more formal structures, but in itself it tends to be informal. To join the "iSchool movement" should thus not necessarily mean becoming an iSchool in any formal sense. Instead, the iSchool movement can be found in relation to epistemology and certain defined research objects which co-exist in a distinct way so as to form what is talked about (only) within the movement as the "iField." An organization such as the iSchools Organization is, however, by definition exclusive. Mission and ethos are tied to certain economic and managerial criteria for membership. These criteria have had to be adjusted as applications from educational environments other than the original North American ones have been granted. In a way, this may be said to be an inclusive strategy, but it is inclusive only on an administrative level. The exclusive character is necessary mainly for three reasons: (1) it facilitates the demarcation of a research area, related to specific societal challenges or business segments that are easily recognizable; this is the so-called "iField"; (2) it sets the parameters for the ability to define certain preferred forms of collaboration, for example between Library and Information Science and computer science, and (3) it helps in creating organizational entities at member universities which may engage in competition for funding, which is sometimes out of reach for more traditional Library and Information Science schools.

The relation between inclusiveness and exclusiveness in iSchools is still a matter of resolve. With too much inclusiveness, branding will become meaningless and perhaps superseded by more established alternatives such as "library schools." With too much exclusiveness, the iSchools Organization runs the risk of becoming a fringe entity, not only in its position between academia and industry, but within specific research fields as the vast majority of Library and Information Science departments and schools do very well without the iSchool label. In order to succeed, it also needs to be able to formulate a problem-based legitimacy that corresponds to current societal challenges which channels priorities from funding agencies and universities. One way of dealing with these problems is to relate the mission of the iSchools Organization to (1) new kinds of academic collaboration, and (2) organizational developments within universities. In doing this, it is important to keep in mind that the iSchools Organization has for a number of years now left its American character behind and now actively strives to be, in a true sense, global.

## *The Art of Professing Inclusive Exclusiveness*

On the iSchools website, the terms iSchool Movement, iSchools Organization, iCaucus, iSchool Caucus, and simply iSchools are used in surprisingly non-defined ways.[1] Therefore, to say what is what is sometimes not easy. In its mission statement we find reference to the "iSchool Caucus," which does not exist in other contexts. Perhaps it really does not matter as there are many more complex matters

---

1. iSchools.org

formulated through its somewhat arcane discourse. Let us look at the mission statement in full:

> The iSchool Caucus seeks to maximize the visibility and influence of its member schools, and their interdisciplinary approaches to harnessing the power of information and technology, and maximizing the potential of humans. We envision a future in which the iSchool Movement has spread around the world, and the information field is widely recognized for creating innovative systems and designing information solutions that benefit individuals, organizations, and society. iSchool graduates will fill the personnel and leadership needs of organizations of all types and sizes; and our areas of research and inquiry will attract strong support and have profound impacts on society and on the formulation of policy from local to international levels.[2]

This is what iSchools want to do. This is where they want to go. This statement can be divided into four parts. First, there is the statement that this mission is limited to its member schools, that is the iSchools Organization in a narrow sense, not the wider movement. Its aim is to maximize "the potential of humans" through interaction between information and technology. This formulation emphasizes the idea of information as a redeemer and if only used rightly, it will enable humanity to evolve to some sort of new level. Similar messianic ideals are not unusual in more general discussions on the influence of information on society. On the contrary, they can be found in numerous treatises as diverse as Alvin Toffler's *The Third Wave*[3] and the more recent

---

2. iSchools.org

3. Alvin Toffler, *The Third Wave* (New York: Bantam, 1980).

*The 4th Revolution* by Luciano Floridi.[4] Second, a vision of the future is provided in which information connected to innovation, design, and solutions becomes beneficial to individuals, organizations, and society. Third, graduates from the affiliated schools should be expected to emerge as members and leaders in "organizations of all types and sizes." Finally, the statement establishes the political significance of the organization. But what legislation and social movements the organization wishes to influence are not specified.

This mission statement calls for some further consideration. One of the most enigmatic issues surrounding iSchools is the use of the term "information." One could assume that there is a clear working definition to take as a point of departure within the organization, not least since there is an "iField" posited that is to be studied and developed. However, there is no such definition to be found. Instead, looking at the writings of some of the most influential thinkers within the organization, the information concept becomes not only interesting, but surprisingly arcane. In a 2011 piece titled "The Audacious Vision of Information Schools," Harry Bruce, former Dean of the iSchool at University of Washington, has this to say about what his school is studying:

> Information is a 'thing' (content, document, form) with potential value and application that becomes apparent with its use by an individual.... As an object or thing, information can be owned and shared. It can be private, public, open or secure. Information can be represented, catalogued, classified, organized, and stored. It can be enhanced by re-structuring,

---

4. Luciano Floridi, *The 4th Revolution: How the Infosphere is Reshaping Human Reality* (Oxford, UK: Oxford University Press, 2014).

packaging, abstracting and indexing. Information has value. It is needed by organizations and individuals. When it is used, information can alter an individual's knowledge structures and facilitate discovery, decision making, and the completion of tasks and projects.[5]

Michael Seadle and Elke Greifeneder of Humboldt University in Berlin, perhaps the most prominent European iSchool, have this to say on the issue: iSchools deal with "not just the paper and media based realms of library collections, but information in the broadest sense that includes potentially everything in the internet and every form of information found in the world."[6] They then go on to make explicit reference to Suzanne Briet's 1951 treatise *Qu'est que-ce la documentation?*, a cornerstone of the European documentation movement which Michael Buckland and Ronald Day, among others, have used to formulate epistemological positions for Library and Information Science as alternatives to the ones based on an all-too-vague information concept. Seadle and Greifeneder continue:

> If iSchool students study documents, then the polar bear baby Knut in the Berlin zoo is not merely an international celebrity, but a document waiting to be read. This kind of breadth is critical to the concept of an iSchool because iSchools break out of library norms and explicitly include everything that might possibly be a source from which we gather both the raw material that goes into our scholarly endeavors and the processed peer-

---

5. Harry Bruce, "The Audacious Vision of Information Schools," *Journal of Library and Information Science* 37 no. 1 (2011): 7.

6. Michael Seadle and Elke Greifeneder, "Envisioning an iSchool Curriculum," *Information Research* 12 no. 4 (2007): paper colise02., n.p.

reviews form that we have long made the exclusive content of research libraries.[7]

This is a bit confusing. In both of these well-known texts, information, the most fundamental badge of legitimacy of the iSchool movement, is defined as, well, a document and the process of documentation. For anyone even vaguely familiar with the ideas and ideals of the European documentation movement, this will come as no surprise. It might even feel consoling, for since Jonathan Furner published his famous paper "Information Science without Information?" fifteen years ago, we should feel more comfortable with any entity other than "information" as the basis for scholarly analysis, and documents/documentation is perhaps that which is most closely at hand.[8] As soon as both Bruce and Seadle and Greifeneder divert from the idea of information as "thing," with reference to Michael Buckland's analysis, or call poor polar bear Knut trapped behind bars in Berlin a "document waiting to be read," the arguments become lost in translation.[9] If information, and thus the iSchool movement, is at the heart of "everything," then it runs the risk of being at the heart of nothing, or at the very least of becoming something which is hard to delineate analytically from knowledge interests better formulated in other scholarly fields. When Bruce points to the "re-structuring, packaging, abstracting and indexing"

---

7. Seadle and Greifeneder, n.p.

8. Jonathan Furner, "Information Studies without Information," *Library Trends* 52, no. 3 (2004): 427-446.

9. Knut died in captivity in 2011, unhappy but commercially successful. The city of Berlin has secured him as a trademark.

of information as a thing (documents), he comes very close to not only a necessary materiality but to what Library and Information Science does and always has done for, and in, professional library practice. Information is like money in that sense; it is an abstraction with no inherent value, that becomes interesting only when tied to a combination of material manifestations and social practices.

Is it thus fair to say that that the iSchool movement or the iSchools Organization is nothing but a collection of library schools with a brand? Yes and no. There are two kinds of iSchools: (1) by far the most common is the often quite large Library and Information Science department which has been upgraded or re-branded into an iSchool, and (2) a growing minority of iSchools that are "compiled" from the start by a combination of disciplines across faculties at a single university, where the iSchool brand acquires the role of a gathering label for interdisciplinary educational programs and research centers. In these, a Library and Information Science department is only one of several contributors. In both types, the task of initiating and implementing new kinds of programs and collaborations under the iField flag is pivotal. Depending on which way the iSchool has formed, these programs vary in outlook although some of the most central problems are shared. John Budd and Catherine Dumas point out these problems, and their possible solutions, in a study on "epistemic multiplicity" in iSchools. They take their departure with the notion that we actually do have something new to deal with here—that the iSchool construct provides an opportunity to manage change through the definition of one or several new epistemic positions.[10] Their way into this

---

10. John M. Budd and Catherine Dumas, "Epistemic Multiplicity in

is as self-evident as it is original: people do not just become interdisciplinary. Creating a new field of research or a new expanded (inter)disciplinary identity is a process which tends to include a good deal of resistance and organizational inertia. The possible obstacles are numerous. Terminology might be unique to certain disciplines and not occur in others and, if they do, they will most likely have different meanings. In an iSchool context, several basic concepts are in need of negotiation before achieving a mutual understanding between, for instance, Library and Information Science, computer science, media and communication studies, and soft systems informatics: just think of "information," "document," "data," "filing," "index," "digital," "humanities," etc. These are terms with more or less distinct meanings in a number of disciplines, which makes them subject to conflicting interpretations during integrative processes, such as the development of new master's level curricula and research programs. Designing a master's program in digital humanities may very well result in a number of courses in humanities being grouped together with more technical "digital" courses without much integration actually happening. At worst this results in a kind of schizophrenic feeling among students who simply don't see the connection. "Successful interdisciplinary collaboration," write Budd and Dumas, "frequently requires some *discomfort*; participants have to be willing to engage in epistemologically challenging assumptions and questions."[11]

---

iSchools: Expanding Knowledge through Interdisciplinarity / La multiplicité épistémic dans les iSchools: le developpement des connaissances grâce à l'interdisciplinarité," *Canadian Journal of Information and Library Science* 38, no. 4 (2014): 271-286.

11. Budd and Dumas, 275. Italics in original.

In order to overcome such discomfort, the authors suggest a semiotic model which can work as a basis for understanding in an explicit negotiation of concepts and models used by partners in interdisciplinary work. Having a core defined in a socially—or commercially—accepted "center" such as an "iField" in an "information society" makes iSchools well prepared to manage such merging. Still, as research has shown, discomfort in interdisciplinary collaboration is not only found between participating disciplines, but within them as well. Ragnar Audunson and Liv Gjestrum have shown this internal skepticism when in 2014 the department of Library and Information Science transformed into an iSchool at what is now the Oslo Metropolitan University in Norway.[12] They point to a number of things that were seen as problematic from the beginning: the movement from (L) to (I) in Library and Information Science, the continued American bias seen not least in the iCaucus, and the self-fostered elitism manifested in the idea that the iSchool brand represents a certain kind of quality. In a country such as Norway, where education in librarianship and Library and Information Science has close and traditional ties to the public library sector, none of these necessarily made the transformation into an iSchool a very attractive option. The L to I movement was seen as unnecessary, the American bias made it seem irrelevant, and the idea of the iSchool logo as a stamp of quality assurance was seen as simply not true as there are no quality criteria for membership. In line with Budd and Dumas' ideas, these are what could be described as organizational discomforts shared

---

12. Ragnar Audunson and Liv Gjestrum, "Bibliotek- og informasjonsfaglig utdanning: Fra etatsskole til iSchool," in *Samle, formidle, dele: 75 år med bibliotekarutdanning*, ed. Ragnar Andreas Audunson, (Oslo: ABM-Media AS, 2015), 11-46.

by many schools when entering the iSchools Organization—perhaps even in the US. The Norwegian experience is shared by other Scandinavian iSchools, as was seen in a workshop at the 2016 iConference in which a host of Norwegian, Swedish, and Danish scholars were actively seeking a way forward with humanistic/social science integrity remaining intact.[13] A study that I did with Koraljka Golub and Lars Seldén indicates similar discomforts in both Scandinavian and American schools, albeit with differences in emphasis.[14]

This last point is interesting, not least in considering why non-American schools and departments should join the iSchools Organization. After all, they ended up doing so in Oslo and they do so in increasing numbers all over the world, my own university included; Linnaeus University has created an "iInstitute," hosting an iSchool of the second type described above, one which I had the privilege of participating in the creation of. Harry Bruce concludes that "[a]ffiliation with the iSchool movement is considered a positive affirmation of the quality and impact of the creative work, scholarship, research and academic program of a member school."[15] Creating an air of attraction is important for any movement, not least in one that wishes to distinguish itself in the form of an organization

---

13. Jack Andersen, Ragnar Andreas Audunson, Svanhild Aabo, Helena Francke, Henrik Jochumsen, and Michael Kristiansson, "Partnership with Society: A Social and Cultural Approach to iSchool-Research" in *Proceedings, iConference 2016*, Philadelphia, PA, https://www.ideals.illinois.edu/bitstream/handle/2142/89445/Andersen496.pdf.

14. Korlajka Golub, Joacim Hansson, and Lars Seldén, "Cult of the 'I': Organizational Symbolism and Curricula in Three Scandinavian iSchools with Comparisons to Three American," *Journal of Documentation* 73, no. 1 (2017): 48-74.

15. Bruce, "The Audacious Vision of Information Schools," 9.

including only a subset of potential members. Again, Seadle and Greifeneder address the issue from another angle, by defining quality in the kind of tasks for which the member schools prepare their students:

> They [iSchools] are not preparing students for today's libraries, but for leadership positions in tomorrow's information infrastructure, which they fully intend to help create. Their mission is transformative. iSchools are training innovators, perhaps even revolutionaries.[16]

Needless to say, they are not talking about political revolutionaries, but entrepreneurial ones. This points to the character of the iSchool movement as it is promoted by the organization itself: inclusive elitism, innovation, and entrepreneurial revolutionaries. We recognize this rhetoric from the ideology behind the entrepreneurial university—what is going on here is also a change of mindset. The vast majority of students in Library and Information Science want to become librarians, but they are treated as if they will become the leadership of "tomorrow's information infrastructure." Do they care? Naturally this is bold organizational rhetoric, but the effect is one which, in many cases, is probably not noticed by the students of librarianship—they continue to maintain their focus and thrive in today's libraries. More importantly, they inspire us to search for the iSchool movement's claim for excellence and quality in another direction—in the light of expectations formulated within the contemporary higher education area. Let me illustrate this by briefly returning once again to university ideology.

---

16. Seadle and Greifeneder, "Envisioning an iSchool Curriculum," n.p.

## *iSchools and the Notion of Structural Accretion*

In order to understand the legitimacy and the *raison d'être* of iSchools, we must look beyond the concrete interdisciplinary ambition of expanding Library and Information Science into the realm of more data science-oriented technical discourses. When doing so, it doesn't suffice to focus on the education of librarians. Instead it is necessary to understand the development of the iSchool movement in relation to what is going on in university policy and management.

The contemporary university, similar to the iSchools Organization, is becoming increasingly global. It thus displays decreased dependency on national or regional differences between bureaucratic cultures and educational systems. In most European countries for example, universities have traditionally existed with significantly less money than their American counterparts. This is due to a number of factors, one of the most important being different traditions regarding the relation between higher education and industry. While much of American higher education is built on private funding, this has been relatively rare in many European countries. The European Union now actively encourages private-public cross-funding, the point of departure being the fact that universities are basically tax funded. This makes, at least in the iSchool environment, for interesting variations in how to achieve the contribution to economic growth that is now the governing principle of higher education on both sides of the Atlantic, as well as in the Asia/Pacific region. The Americanization of the relation between industry and academia leads to a highly competitive environment, with increased demands on rapid project implementation and production of results, followed by immediate accountability.

Stanford sociologist Neil Smelser posits in his book *Dynamics of the Contemporary University: Growth, Accretion, and Conflict,* that the implementation of new departmental structures and interdisciplinary initiatives, of which iSchools may be examples, brings core neoliberal ideals into university practice. The key concept is *structural accretion*. It is used to describe the way universities (in his examples, American ones) change and manage organizational growth. "The idea is simple enough," he writes, "[g]rowth is achieved by adding structures 'on the side' of existing structures, but, critically, older structures are not shed in the process, even though their salience may change. The result is, over time, to create a kind of multifunctional monster with a diversity of structures, roles and groups."[17] This is nowadays not only applicable to American universities but is a significant feature in European ones, too, not least those which brand themselves as entrepreneurial. Multifunctional monsters. There is today a streak of universalism in the processes which materialize the concept of structural accretion. In short this means that academic disciplines and departments, usually consisting of a conglomerate of disciplines living more or less parallel lives, are left untouched. Disciplines are given the role of bedrock in a basic structure where scholars and students can maintain their specific identity, and departments are then given the role of housing disciplines of suitable size to meet the requirements for administrative and managerial efficiency. My own department, the Linnaeus University School of Cultural Sciences, and faculty can serve as a brief example of how complex such a basic structure can be. There

---

17. Neil J. Smelser, *Dynamics of the Contemporary University: Growth, Accretion, and Conflict* (Berkeley, CA: University of California Press, 2013), 40.

is, despite the name of the school, no such thing as "cultural science" at Linnaeus University. Instead, the school is an administrative umbrella construct, consisting of no less than eight well-defined disciplines: History, Philosophy, Religious Studies, Archeology, Geography, Cultural Sociology, Cultural Geography, and Library and Information Science. Each works with a high degree of autonomy, and although a running seminar drawing participants from the various disciplines exists, the focus among scholars remains on their disciplinary identity. The school currently offers a master's program in "cultural science," but this only engages four of the eight disciplines: Library and Information Science, Archeology, Religious Studies, and History. Admission and graduation are tied to each of the disciplines involved. The School of Cultural Sciences is part of the Faculty for Arts and Humanities, consisting of an additional seven schools or institutions built, in various ways, by related but parallel disciplines covering everything from a well renowned design school to film, literature, journalism, and a large variety of language studies. It is on this level, the faculty level, that most management and administration duties are placed.

This is by no means an unusual situation. The combination of disciplines within the departmental structure is purely random. Every university has its own version of a cultural science department, or sometimes in our field, a GLAM department combining archival science, Library and Information Science, and museology. The thing is, as pointed out by Smelser, this is not where growth and development take place—at least it is not supposed to. Instead Linnaeus University, as do most others, builds alternative structures aimed specifically at meeting demands for vehicularity, flexibility, and interdisciplinarity. What Smelser does brilliantly is to show the dynamics between these two parallel structures or systems. The traditional discipline-based institutional structure represents a kind of inertia through its stability. It is important to remember here that scientific disciplines as we know them are manifestations of a division of knowledge made up to meet the social and epistemological requirements of mid-19th-century Europe. The second structure consists of research centers, interdisciplinary groups, and schools, founded to meet the societal challenges or specific problems areas of today. Quite often these are defined outside of academia and should therefore be seen as kinds of response structures. They are important as they influence all parts of university life: leadership, shared governance, competitiveness, funding application practices, administrative power, and relations to external patrons. They are the practical response from higher education institutions to meeting ideological shifts in research policies. iSchools are parts of such a response. Depending on which of the two versions of iSchools we are talking about, the character of this response differs, or at least seems to. In what way can iSchools based on traditional library schools be said to be a part of the "monster" that Smelser speaks of? And, what are the consequences of letting go of the library school model in forming an iSchool, as seen from an educational perspective? In short, how are the structures in universities bridged in the case of iSchools?

In order to make sense of this we need to consider the distinction between educational levels and research. Structural accretion tends to reduce the connection of basic program offerings by individual disciplines and the activities of interdisciplinary research centers or schools. In European higher education, the gulf runs between the two main levels defined by the Bologna Declaration: the undergraduate and the graduate. The focus is not on undergraduate program development, but entirely on graduate and research levels. This has been observed on several occasions in the Library and Information Science literature. Laurie Bonnici, Manimegalai Subramaniam, and Kathleen Burnett conclude in an analysis of American iCaucus schools with master programs accredited by the American Library Association, that very limited shifts in focus have taken place over time in the transition from library schools to iSchools. The iField is said to have simply "ingested the L" of the discipline.[18] In a similar kind of study, Heting Chu concludes that "it lacks of supporting evidence…to define iSchools as a group fundamentally different from or superior to non-iSchools in library and information science education."[19] The previously mentioned article that I co-authored with my department colleagues Koraljka Golub and Lars Seldén confirms this as well, which included three Scandinavian iSchools along with three American ones in an analysis of six schools with a combined total of 427 courses on the graduate (master's) level.[20] The fact is that the only real differences seen are due to program construction, with American schools having a significantly larger number of individual course options in

---

18. Laurie J. Bonnici, Manimegalai M. Subramaniam and Kathleen Burnett, "Everything Old is New Again: The Evolution of Library and Information Science Education from LIS to iField," *Journal of Education for Library and Information Science* 50, no. 4 (2009): 263-274.

19. Heting Chu (2012) "iSchools and Non-iSchools in the USA: An Examination of their Master's Programs," *Education for Information* 29 (2012): 1-17.

20. Golub, Hansson and Seldén, "Cult of the 'I'", 56-57.

their programs than Scandinavian schools do. This unveils the fact that the iSchools Organization is not only not necessarily one to influence Library and Information Science on the undergraduate level, but it seemingly also does not do so even on the master's tier of the graduate level.

## *Example: Horizon 2020—The iField Materialized?*

If there is little support for the iSchool movement making an actual impact on Library and Information Science on the educational level, there surely must be one in research. The iSchool movement relates heavily to contemporary research agendas, such as the European Union's Horizon 2020 and other large-scale initiatives addressing a wide variety of societal challenges through research and innovation in the cross-sectional space between academia and industry. Horizon 2020 is a close to 80-billion-Euro structure into which constructs like the entrepreneurial university are exclusively made to fit.[21] The mission statement of Horizon 2020, in its aim to secure Europe's global competitiveness, looks like this:

> Seen as a means to drive economic growth and create jobs, Horizon 2020 has the political backing of Europe's leaders and the Members of the European Parliament. They agreed that research is an investment in our future and so put it at the heart of the EU's blueprint for smart, sustainable and inclusive growth and jobs. By coupling research and innovation, Horizon 2020 is helping to achieve this with its emphasis on excellent science, industrial leadership and tackling societal challenges. The goal is to ensure Europe produces world-class science, removes barriers to innovation and makes it easier for

---

21. The funding total for Horizon 2020 is to be distributed over a seven-year period between 2014 and 2020.

the public and private sectors to work together in delivering innovation. Horizon 2020 is open to everyone, with a simple structure that reduces red tape and time so participants can focus on what is really important. This approach makes sure new projects get off the ground quickly—and achieve results faster.[22]

Everything I have discussed so far is here seen in action: the equation between economic growth and social/democratic development, the coupling of academia and business (research and innovation), knowledge creation as production, the drive to reduce bureaucratic obstacles, and the emphasis on speed in project implementation for "faster" achievement of results. As Horizon 2020 is one of the largest research funding initiatives in the world right now, its construction matters in ways that go well beyond the content of research being negotiated in universities and industry. Looking at the variety of research areas that are covered, Horizon 2020 displays three features that include every aspect of this particular advocacy of combining research and innovation: (1) ubiquitous ICT (information and communication technology) development permeating all aspects of research and social development, (2) emphasis on multi-disciplinary research, and (3) the notion that public institutions should be developed through private enterprise initiatives and solutions. With the risk of exaggerating, one might say that the public sector is the problem and industrial ICT-related innovation is the pre-determined solution. This is the way in which economic growth and democratic development is treated as equivalent: text-book neoliberalism.

---

22. https://ec.europa.eu/programmes/horizon2020/en/what-horizon-2020.

Having iSchools in mind, as we do here, there are of course a number of research areas within Horizon 2020 that could be of interest, as many can be reduced to the point where information technology and society intersect. Of the twenty-three research areas categorized by the initiative, several seem, at first glance, to allow the iSchool agenda and Horizon 2020 to meet. Three of these are "ICT research and innovation," "Society," and "Social sciences and the humanities." No matter which areas we look at, information, knowledge, and technology are at center—all in order to "boost the productivity puzzle" of Europe. In the area of "Society," the main goals focus on increasing the perceived social relevance of scientific knowledge and getting people more engaged in research activities, be that by encouraging kids to play at science centers or increasing the publication of research through scholarly open access. One of the prime focus points is to "integrate society in science and innovation issues, policies and activities in order to integrate citizens' interests and values and to increase the quality, relevance, social acceptability and sustainability of research and innovation outcomes in various fields of activity from social innovation to areas such as biotechnology and nanotechnology." This is also under the heading of "Society." Of course, there is nothing bad or even misguided in making people aware of, and take part in, scientific progress, but it is interesting to consider the formulation as an example of the kind of discourse we are dealing with here. In the category of social sciences and the humanities, the program lists five main areas of interest: (1) health, demographic change, and wellbeing, (2) smart, green, and integrated transport, (3) climate action and resource efficiency, (4) Europe in a changing world, and

(5) leadership in enabling and industrial technology.[23] This is not exactly your traditional humanities department, but this is about as humanistic as the EU gets these days. Let me briefly consider one of the areas that has drawn the attention of library research scholars: "Europe in a changing world." The introduction to this research area reads: "[T]here will be a range of topics covering areas like new ideas, strategies and governance structures for overcoming the crisis in Europe, innovation in the public sector enabled by ICT, business model innovation, social innovation, European cultural heritage, history, culture and identity."

The basic premise here is that there is a *crisis* in Europe, and indeed there are a number of issues that are in need of careful consideration, primarily perhaps the current rise of right-wing populist nationalism and its challenge to democratic institutions and systems. It is however highly uncertain what crisis we are dealing with here. Not unexpectedly, the public sector seems to be one in need of innovative information technologies and new business models. One might argue that the position given to the humanities and social sciences within the European research community is so reductionistic that its value can only be defined against the backdrop of the priority for the entrepreneurial creation of incentives for innovation. Within the cultural heritage area, where I have been an assigned proposal reviewer for several years now, awareness of this is so great that virtually no research proposals are submitted that do not focus on digitization efforts, mostly through collaboration between humanist scholars and software developing companies—otherwise, no

---

23. Horizon 2020, Social Sciences and Humanities, https://ec.europa.eu/programmes/horizon2020/en/area/social-sciences-and-humanities.

funding will be granted. Indeed, there might be some mutual benefit here, but it definitely directs scholarly practice in a way which excludes as many important research questions as it opens up to new ones. But then again, who is to decide what knowledge is desired at a certain point in time, and who is to cast doubt over the apparent priority of start-up companies trying out new applications with the legitimacy of scientific affiliations? The same goes the other way around, not least in the cultural or, for that matter, the educational sciences—*create an app*, the mantra says, and gain scientific legitimacy through connection with innovative enterprise. The world is, after all seamlessly digital, isn't it? At least this is a discourse that the iSchools Organization is more than willing to promote. The question is, does it matter? Does the iSchool label actually do any good in the eyes of the reviewers in initiatives like Horizon 2020? It is doubtful that it does and the reason is simple—research policy in the European Union is problem-oriented. Perhaps never before (although that may be argued) has research been politically directed more explicitly than today, both in terms of perspectives and content. Who performs the research activities is not important as long as it gets done and as long as it gets the economic wheels spinning. Even a very brief look at the Horizon 2020 projects granted to Library and Information Science departments points to this problem.

During the last couple of years, two major projects have been initiated with Swedish Library and Information Science institutions involved—one without iSchool participation and one with. As part of the program "Fostering new skills by means of excellent initial training of new researchers,"[24]

---

24. H2020-EU.1.3.1.

*Participatory Memory Practices. Concepts, strategies, and media infrastructures for envisioning socially inclusive potential futures of European Societies through culture" (POEM)* is a project that aims at developing strategies, practices, and infrastructures for a "socially inclusive public memory" as a reply to "growing nationalism and islamist radicalization."[25] Under the call for "Information and Communication Technology," the project *Smart, Userfriendly, Interactive, Tactual, Cognition-Enhancer that Yields Extended Sensosphere* (SUITCEYES) not only displays acronymic brilliance, but more importantly works to increase social participation for 2.5 million deafblind persons in the EU through a haptic intelligent personalized interface (HIPI).[26] POEM focuses on training doctoral students in the field of cultural heritage studies and SUITCEYES focuses on product development. Despite their differences they are two very typical Horizon 2020 projects with a notable presence of Library and Information Science. In SUITCEYES, a seven-institution consortium has been formed with the Swedish School of Library and Information Science at the University of Borås, the biggest iSchool in Sweden, as the administrative hub. POEM consists of seven departments from five countries, with Swedish participation from the Department of ALM at Uppsala University.

Both of these projects are well conceived and worthy recipients of the acquired funding, and my point here is by no means to criticize the projects themselves or the people involved. What I instead want to bring attention to is the

---

25. https://www.ne-mo.org/news/article/nc/1/browse/3/nemo/13-phd-positions-in-the-eu-horizon-2020-marie-sklodowska-curie-project-msca-etn-poem/418.html

26. http://suitceyes.eu/

manifestation of the interest and ideology of the whole Horizon 2020 initiative as seen through these concrete projects. As mentioned, one of the points of departure for the Horizon 2020 agenda is the idea that Europe is in crisis, without specifying what kind. It is through the implementation of research that this becomes clear. In the cultural heritage area there are two main current movements that need to be dealt with, as seen in the POEM description: "growing nationalism and islamist radicalization." Both are definitely in need of scientific analysis and of political interest, but they are of very different kinds. The fact that right-wing nationalist parties and movements are currently attracting large groups of voters all over Europe is in its most basic analysis a consequence of popular discontent over decades of imposing a neoliberal agenda in the EU and its inherent confusion between economic logic and social progression. Paradoxically this has led to, not a growing progressive movement, but instead a right-wing turn ripe with nostalgic sentiments as seen in examples such as Brexit and the perhaps less flamboyant re-writing of Swedish history in *Sverigedemokraterna*'s appropriation of the 1950s Swedish version of the welfare state—all the way to the point where its pioneers are being portrayed as representing today's nationalist drive for a monocultural society. However, these pioneers of the welfare state were never even close to being right-wing populists; in most cases, they were social-democrats. Historical revision is an explicit strategy seen not least in cultural heritage policy as highlighted in POEM. To place this on the same level as "islamist radicalization" is problematic. Seen beside the political and hate-motivated violence by right-wing populist movements, Islamist radicalization in Europe can only be described as a fringe phenomenon enhanced by a discourse of fear. That this is portrayed as a threat to "European values" *within* Europe is part of discourse initiated and fueled by the far right. "European values" are, if any such actually exist in a uniform sense, definitely under pressure today, but hardly from the Muslim community. Instead the forces that have been unleashed by the very ideology sparking huge initiatives such as Horizon 2020 come into play. We find ourselves in the midst of a circular process from which it is hard to see a way out.

If POEM highlights politically sensitive and complex issues by equating social causes and effects, SUITCEYES displays a completely different and more straightforward example of the entrepreneurial spirit in research. Apart from the obviously well-guided and emancipatory aim to facilitate life and social participation for a marginalized group in society, there is a commercial inducement which is, at the end of the day, the most important. The emancipatory aspect of the project is relying on its commercial potential. Needs of the target group are analyzed in order for a technological development and utilization to take place. The exploitation part of the project which runs in parallel to the technological development of, among other things, smart textiles aims to "analyse the environment in which the SUITCEYES results will be used in terms of applicability to the targeted user community, conformance to regulations, market opportunities and finally to develop a business strategy able to bring this innovative system successfully into the market."[27] It is not enough to develop solutions for increased quality of life for a severely disadvantaged group in society; the success of the project depends instead on its ability to meet the

---

27. Work-package 8: http://suitceyes.eu/work-packages/.

expectations of "the market." The project is therefore in no real sense emancipatory, as it objectifies its target group in order to achieve market satisfaction. In the end, the deafblind community becomes nothing more than a customer segment for the ever-so-benevolent entrepreneurs who have the primary goal of creating economic revenue.

## *iSchools—Who Needs Them?*

This brief excursion into the ideas and implementation of Horizon 2020 exemplifies a research environment which is very much aligned with the way the iSchool movement presents itself. Basically, this is the kind of environment that the iSchool brand is constructed to function in. It is significant that "inclusion" (not emancipation) is used frequently to underline the fact that we are not dealing with the robber-baron mentality of the Gilded Age, but instead with nice entrepreneurs who use technology as a tool for local and global altruism. Information is good, and information and information technology schools must therefore be the institutional epitome of goodness. But then again, if information is reduced to everything, the iField is not only close to impossible to define but reduced to uselessness. The two examples from Horizon 2020—I could have chosen any others, as many of them carry the same elements—are well suited for iSchool engagement. There is, however, nothing which indicates that the participation of an iSchool makes any difference. This must be seen as a problem within the movement. It is, however not one which is necessarily unexpected. If we return to Smelser's arguments concerning structural accretion, the inertia of departmental and discipline-based structures in research is largely due to the current emphasis on challenges, which rhetorically indicates a discourse close to that of reality TV competitions such as *The Apprentice* and many others. The structures that are built to take on these challenges all have in common a strong goal orientation. In entrepreneurial learning and research environments, goals refer to societal and other challenges only in as much as they are tied to direct applications and economic contributions. Direct applications require that agents outside of academia formulate problems; such agents are often industry representatives, or private or public funding agencies. If the latter, they necessarily formulate politically-defined problems and if the former, commercially-defined ones. Economic contributions are measured and evaluated as research impact. As long as this kind of agenda dominates the research environment globally, the option for individual and social emancipation through research and education is highly limited. This is where the education of librarians comes into this equation. As the iSchools Organization has "ingested" the L in Library and Information Science and coupled up with the information industry—a coupling which is far more important to the iSchools Organization than it is to the information industry—the interpretative prerogative will be that of the information industry. It is no coincidence that the 2019 iConference has as its theme "Inform, Include, Inspire," with Google paying for the keynote speaker. This is a deceptive inclusion where people are treated like customers in an information education-industry cluster which defines social structures as obsolete and the public sector is seen, as it also is in Horizon 2020, as being in need of "new business models." From a Library and Information Science perspective, this is by no means unproblematic. If we agree that librarianship as a profession, and libraries as social institutions, are at the epicenter of the legitimacy of the discipline, then the need for new and entrepreneurial business models should be met with skepticism. When political discourse emphasizes restructuring or innovation in the public sector what is usually meant is, in John Buschman's term, dismantling. When librarians—and library educators—speak of emancipation, what is usually meant is something very different from the information industry's talk of "inclusion." The former is based on a specific set of values and the latter provides an attempt to define ever more finely-tuned customer segments. Inclusion, as opposed to emancipation, further implies a strong element of social control. The question is why the iSchools Organization wants to be part of the information industry discourse and why it needs to define itself in terms of contributors to what the EU speaks of as "the productivity puzzle." However well it works, iSchoolers will only be allowed to sit at the far end of the table and there, the only ones left to brag to are the waiters. Meanwhile, Library and Information Science departments outside of the organization, or the movement, are largely unconcerned. They find their legitimacy elsewhere.

So, what to do with all this? After all, iSchools are here and they are not likely to go anywhere in the foreseeable future; on the contrary. One alternative is to stay out, or opt out, of the iSchools Organization, arguing that it represents a fringe movement and a misguided attempt to meet the basic requirements of increasing international demands for structural accretion in higher education and research. Another alternative is to realize that despite being a fringe movement in academia, there is a large number of influential and creative scholars working within the iSchool movement simply by force of their institutional affiliation. This is an important fact to recognize as structural accretion often develops against a backdrop of inertia of which the working researchers are important parts. That you work in an iSchool does not mean that you on an individual level agree with the objectives of the organization. As an intellectual, one has the obligation to stand as autonomous in relation to one's own department's goals. The fact that Library and Information Science has its legitimacy in relation to professional librarianship and all the practices surrounding it opens up possibilities for scientific work which addresses social issues in ways other than those shown in the Horizon 2020 examples. As most students in Library and Information Science still want to become librarians, and there are no signs to indicate that this will be any different in the years ahead, it becomes important to establish a relationship between the value base of the library profession and the ideology behind the educational system of which they are a part. Students learn the language of capitalism, but they will work in settings largely defying it not only on a discursive level, but in practice as well. Societal challenges may be defined on international levels within or outside of organizations like the European Union; solutions are, however, often local. For librarians, this means community engagement, emancipatory instruction, and the guarding of free information and knowledge access without having the "customer" perspective. In the iSchools Organization, there is no emancipatory or even democratic motivation whatsoever, but in the practices of its member departments these may still be taught and studied by force of the actual grounds for legitimacy and identity of its most central discipline.

So, if the iSchool brand doesn't make any difference, either on the educational program level or in research, then who is asking for it and why? The simplest but perhaps hardest answer is that the iSchools Organization is a club for academic self-indulgence professing its own excellence in a field that does not really exist. If this a correct interpretation, would it not render the organization and the movement completely superfluous? Well, perhaps, but not necessarily. There may still be value in the new arenas for discussion and display of new applied research, such as is seen at the iConference. Having said that, the iConference has significant problems holding up a value of its own beside the more established scientific conferences in Library and Information Science, such as the ASIS&T Annual Meeting, CoLIS, and ISIC, all of which are bringing together much of what is talked about as the iField in more concentrated and intellectually sustainable ways. It can also be of value to have an organization within a discipline that can tap into the current discussion and adopt the discourse of higher education policy at an international level. This is important in the information field as it, if any, transcends national and regional restrictions, forging a gold standard of neoliberal practice that combines the idea of the socially benevolent entrepreneur with crass capitalist logic. Google, the close and revered collaborator with the iConference, removed its famous "Don't Be Evil" motto from its code of conduct in spring of 2018;[28] this is merely an adjustment to what is today general knowledge about the company as well as the information industry at large.

In order to not only maintain, but develop, a critical awareness among students, researchers, and librarians of all sorts concerning the nature of the information industry, insight into its logic and discourse is necessary. It is also something

---

28. Lulu Chang, "Google Eliminated that 'Don't Be Evil' Motto," *Digital Trends* 21 May 2018.

which holds legitimacy in higher education constructs such as the entrepreneurial university. A good way of achieving the desired connection to the neoliberal narrative is to become a part of it, and that is perhaps the most intrinsic value we see when looking at the iSchools Organization in its attempts to become something other than Library and Information Science with a brand. Does it do any good for the education of librarians? Is that even a relevant question? Even if libraries as (information) institutions are mentioned in several places in the context of the iSchools Organization's website, they are clearly not the focus of interest. Rather, it is baggage that needs to be held on to for a while longer, in order to maintain a material legitimacy. In the next and final chapter, I will suggest how the education of librarians and library research can maintain and develop a perspective which takes on vantage points other than those currently governing higher education. These vantage points will allow us to connect to the fundamental values of the profession, and through this create a progressive agenda for social emancipation through the right to free information and knowledge.

## Chapter 6

### EDUCATION FOR LIBRARIANSHIP—MOVING FORWARD

In her essay "The Neoliberal Library," Maura Seale paints a picture of American librarianship as being unable to foster an alternative to the discourse of economism and the reduction of citizens to consumers and customers. Therefore, the profession is willing to uncritically give up the ideals on which it was built. She uses the example of the discourse of information literacy as being particularly vulnerable to neoliberal sentiments in that it is concerned with the educational aspects of the profession which, as in any educational setting, can never be treated as value-free. She concludes that neoliberal discourse aligns librarianship with an ideology that is designed to decrease the importance of social justice, and instead prioritizes subversion of democracy, dismantling of social services, consolidation of the power of economic and political elites, and feeds on the creation of a class of disposable workers.[1] This is a serious criticism that has consequences for librarianship education as well. Her analysis of information literacy guidelines and their implication for

---

1. Maura Seale, "The Neoliberal Library" in *Information Literacy and Social Justice: Radical Professional Practice*, eds. Lua Gregory and Shana Higgins (Sacramento, CA: Library Juice Press, 2013), 58.

professional practice shows how integrated Stuart Sutton and Nancy van House's recommendations in the Panda Syndrome articles from the late 1990's have become in daily professional practice. As I pointed out earlier, in chapters 1 and 2, they suggest a move towards a more market- and business-oriented discourse and practice within both professional librarianship and Library and Information Science. One argument for such an adjustment is the fact that the industrial for-profit sector and the growing educational sector (in which both Library and Information Science and a significant part of library practice are situated) converge by submission to a market-oriented logic. In such environments, issues like democracy, diversity, and social regulation form blocks of inertia, bound to be overcome by inevitable deregulation. For all it is worth, these sentiments have dominated the observations in this essay as well, whether concerning the creation of the entrepreneurial university or the iField discourse.

That we are now in a place where libraries and librarianship, perhaps for the first time ever, are connected to power structures that are not to their benefit is hardly a controversial statement to make. The "contract" between librarianship and the ruling power that was suggested in the first chapter of this essay is, at least in part, broken. In many countries, librarians have to work at odds with their governing bodies by means of their professional ethos and the positive weight of tradition. Within the neoliberal agenda, libraries have to legitimize their existence and contributions to social progress through criteria not in alignment with their practices. Seale ends her essay by underlining the need for library instruction, and librarianship at large, to "begin promoting an awareness of the field's embeddedness within a neoliberal political and economic context in order to open up a discursive space in which alternatives to neoliberalism can be conceptualized and implemented."[2] Given the probable fact that the neoliberal hegemony will not likely disappear in any foreseeable future, this is indeed a challenging call to arms, well worth following in as many ways as possible. My own take on this is built on the idea that it is necessary for librarianship to create an identity promoting emancipatory resilience. By this I mean that it is important to always emphasize that libraries and librarianship are not a good fit for the current ideological hegemony, but they are still a necessity for society. As a concept, emancipatory resilience summarizes a path that librarianship can present as a viable alternative. An important way of consolidating such a position is to develop a supporting educational structure through Library and Information Science. Neoliberal ideology definitely has a grip on the profession, but so does a fundamentally emancipatory self-image and deeply rooted identity which has developed within the profession over a long period of time. It is possible to unearth this with the proper theoretical and methodological tools—my suggestions for two such tools are the theory of recognition of the other in social conflict and the theory of agonistic pluralism. Claiming and exposing this identity is, however, not enough. We need to find a way to address future discussions on the tension between external legitimacy and internal identity, both in practice and in education. This tension will most certainly become more accentuated over the coming years. In order to try to achieve this, Library and Information Science finds itself in a tug-of-war between possible loyalties. The scholars of the discipline need to align themselves with the neoliberal

---

2. Seale, 58-59.

educational discourse and through this reform librarianship as a profession by encouraging librarians to find their place in the ever growing "productivity puzzle." Or, they need to stand loyal to the basic premises and ethos of librarianship as an emancipatory profession and, by doing so, align it with a set of educational ideals more in line with those I have shown formulated in the *Magna Charta Universitatum*. Does the choice matter? I believe that it does; the direction taken by education for librarianship influences the direction of the practice in several ways. How this should be done is of course open for debate. I suggest focusing on three main areas which are valuable when formulating a long-term alternative to the neoliberal ideology. In order to develop an educational program for strong and resilient librarianship within the established disciplinary frame of Library and Information Science, the focus should be on: (1) critical analysis of the fundamental concepts of librarianship with the goal of creating an alternative to the present discourse, (2) connecting librarianship and the education of librarians to discussions about the role of the humanities in society and in the higher education area, and (3) creating an emancipatory narrative about the ethos of librarianship that will be strong enough to maintain its long-term social relevance.

## *Revising Concepts, Revising Discourse*

Library and Information Science has always been at odds with its most fundamental concepts. To have a clear conceptual foundation is necessary in order to delineate areas of knowledge interest, concrete research problems, and what contributions can be made to cross-disciplinary research environments. It is telling that, as the name "Library and Information Science" implies, there are two complementary directions within the discipline: one focusing on the concept of information and one focusing on perspectives geared toward institutions and the profession. For the most part during the last forty years or so, conceptual discussions have circled, almost exclusively, around the former. The library science part happens to have a very straightforward legitimacy and social relevance, with a strong connection to both scholarly inquiry and social practice. Bernd Frohmann points to an important issue when he notices that "the contingent, local character of laboratory resources and results is one of the most important findings in recent studies of scientific practice. Yet [...] scientific results are articulated as phenomena that are informative in contexts beyond those of their production; they speak with the voice of nature, not humanity."[3] On a conceptual level, this is also valid for the "i" part of Library and Information Science. The claim for universalism in information processes and the elusiveness of information as a concept have created an insecurity in the discipline which constructions such as the "iField" have attempted to overcome. This insecurity is central to the paradigmatic discussions of the discipline, primarily affecting a couple of the more dominant paradigms that have made more or less explicit hegemonic claims. The most obvious example is the so-called "cognitive viewpoint," which was allowed to dominate the discourse on "users" for well over two decades, until various alternatives emerged in the late 1990s and early 2000s.

The problem with the cognitive paradigm was not in the use of established models from "real" cognitive science disciplines, but rather in the ways they were combined

---

3. Bernd Frohmann, *Deflating Information: From Science Studies to Documentation* (Toronto: Toronto University Press, 2004), 199.

with the concept of information. This was mostly done through an acceptance of the classical mathematical theory of communication, first presented by Claude Shannon and Warren Weaver in 1949.[4] Simply put, this model consists of a message that is transmitted from a sender to a receiver in a clinical process. Any disturbances are placed in a "noise" category in the mathematical sense of the term. Applied to the complex situation of information practices, for example a reference interview with a student in a university library, this noise category has a tendency to grow and contain everything that is external to the "clinical" communication process, such as the student's chosen discipline, the student's (and librarian's) place in life, the institutional setting (school, department, university)—in short, anything social. The cognitive viewpoint took this model and transferred it into a model for human information behavior. In the end, however, the negligence of a social dimension in user studies came to a dead end and alternative approaches emerged, not so much as an anti-hegemonic movement as out of necessity. The results, in terms of search tools and understanding the complexity of needs and behavior that naturally characterize any search process, simply needed more dimensions. The need for a redirection of research interests took aim not only at the cognitive framework, which was easy enough to replace by other more appropriate ones, but at the core concept of information as well. Several books on the subject came out at the turn of the last century, such as Scott Lash's *Critique of Information*[5] and, perhaps most prominently, *The*

---

4. Claude Shannon and Warren Weaver, *The Mathematical Theory of Communication* (Urbana: University of Illinois Press, 1963).

5. Scott Lash, *Critique of Information* (London: Sage, 2002).

*Modern Invention of Information: Discourse History and Power* by Ronald Day.[6] Both take their departure from European philosophical critiques of the contemporary as formulated in the first decades of the 20th century by thinkers such as Martin Heidegger and Walter Benjamin. Both translate these critiques into the situation of our own time. We recognize the elements: speed, technological overtake, the idea of the modern as hostile to something essentially human (exemplified for instance by the arguably elitist concept of *le flaneur*). However, while Lash leaves the argument at that, Day takes it further into the realm of contemporary Library and Information Science. He argues that these philosophical excursions provide a point of departure for not just a critique of the contemporary but also for a way out of "the conduit metaphor" used to describe Shannon and Weaver's theory. In an important passage he writes:

> [t]he problem with understanding the conduit metaphor as a model for a political or social state is that it models an ideological prescription, not a reality for either being or community. Consequently, social policy and research projects that are predicated on its social goals and epistemological foundations should be more critically examined than they are at present. A thorough critique of the conduit metaphor, for example, both in terms of its own logical presuppositions and in terms of its political and social functions, would lead one to question the foundations and purposes of many social and 'user centered' studies in information and communication research.[7]

---

6. Ronald E. Day, *The Modern Invention of Information: Discourse, History and Power* (Carbondale, IL: Southern Illinois University Press, 2001)..

7. Day, 59.

What Day calls for here is basically the need to identify a new kind of materiality in the study of information. The main road still leads us towards an understanding of the concept which creates discursive connections to a basically capitalist logic, as pointed out by Frohmann,[8] and which one may today argue replaces the assumed object of study (the user) with the assumed need of the provider (the information industry) as the basis for analysis—a perspective we now see emphasized through the iSchool movement. So, what would an alternative look like? How could we connect education with practice if information is insufficient as a fundamental concept?

The suggestion brought forward by Day comes as part of a growing consciousness of the early documentation movement in Europe. This has led to new ways of thinking about the relation between documentation practices such as metadata and subject analysis—with the concrete example of the Universal Decimal Classification as the "fulfilment" of the intentions of Melvil Dewey—and public access to scholarly knowledge and publications. I will not here discuss this in further detail, as it has been chronicled and analyzed by many others already.[9] Instead I will bring attention to the idea that assigning an increased materiality to the study of information would not only provide an alternative perspective on Library and Information Science, but would indeed provide a more

---

8. Bernd Frohmann, "The Power of Images: A Discourse Analysis of the Cognitive Viewpoint," *Journal of Documentation* 48, no. 4 (1992): 365-386.

9. W. Boyd Rayward, "The Origins of Information Science and the International Institute of Bibliography/International Federation for Information and Documentation (FID)," *Journal of the American Society for Information Science* 48, no. 4 (1997): 289-300; Michael Buckland, "What is a Document?" *Journal of the American Society for Information Science* 48, no. 9 (1997): 804-809.

pertinent connection between the discipline and the library profession—and in a way which aligns more with the ethos of the profession than the current developments do.

While any kind of definition of information lands outside of the discipline and needs to be adjusted, document and documentation processes can be said to be at the center of librarianship in a way which also make extra-disciplinary theorizing resonate in a different way, simply because there is a unique identity in the practice of documentation that is positioned at the intersection of librarianship and scholarly communication. This may, however, be widened into a larger social context as well. In doing so, one effort that has gained specific attention from the documentation study community within Library and Information Science is the treatise *Documentality: Why It is Necessary to Leave Traces* by the Italian philosopher Maurizio Ferraris.[10] His approach is ontological. In opposition to the familiar trope of the information society, he instead suggests that documents and documentation processes have such profound impact on the organization of society, and on institutions and social processes, that it is possible to set up an axiom which basically embraces the complete social construct. It says, "Social object = inscribed act," thus creating social objects as well as social processes by means of documents and documentation. Through this, Ferraris manages to build a manifest, material alternative to the fluid and abstract idea of the information society. By relying on documents and documentation processes, it also becomes possible to create an alternative take on the inherently neoliberal character of the information society, as

---

10. Maurizio Ferraris, *Documentality: Why It is Necessary to Leave Traces* (New York: Fordham Univeristy Press, 2013).

information is seen first and foremost as something which not only can be organized but, more importantly, bought. In the previous chapter's discussion of the iSchool movement's struggle with the information concept, we could see a surprisingly overt reference to documentation; information needs something tangible to cling on to in order to be able to talk about it as a cornerstone of society. In the context of Library and Information Science and librarianship, this cornerstone is the document and the organization of document collections, physical and digital. Based on this, a view of social institutions can be developed. Ferraris does so with help of examples that are simple enough, such as the passport and the practice of mapping the world. The example of national maps is interesting because it is so clear-cut. The documentation, demarcation, and naming of exact land and sea masses can only be obtained through establishing individual documents (maps) that are part of a complex, standardized documentary structure used to legitimize everything from the ownership of natural resources to political and religious power. Documents are also used to fix human memory and to facilitate active communication—a double function that permeates all documents, as also noted by David Levy;[11] just think of notes, poems, letters, newspapers, websites, social media postings, an antelope in a zoo, court verdicts, receipts, scientific articles, graffiti, road signs, engravings, cave paintings, tombstones, the worrying flash of an oil level indicator in your car, ballots, constitutions, and tattoos—to only mention a few. Every single document contains information, but without the context, the intention,

---

11. David M. Levy, *Scrolling Forward: Making Sense of Documents in the Digital Age* (New York: Arcade Publishing, 2001).

and the documentation process that categorizes and provides the documents with meaning, legitimacy, and significance, that inherent information would remain an abstraction. It is this abstraction that the information discourse in Library and Information Science is now built upon and it is what constitutes the basis of the iField and the iSchool movement. In order to gain relevance and legitimacy the movement has sufficed with a general, contextual reductionism adhering to the information industry's economistic approach to information as a currency or a product. This is why libraries are sometimes referred to as part of the information industry. By referring to documentation, librarianship finds a much more relevant context for its identity. This does not mean a reduction of libraries to being just memory institutions; on the contrary. By arguing for the ontological character of documentation, the ordering of documents and the provision of equal and relevant access to documents, public librarianship at least would secure its place in the very fabric of society in a relevant and sustainable way.[12]

Now, here is where most librarians would object by saying that their libraries are so much more than their collections and of course they are right. But they would not be library institutions if the collections and the dynamics of document collections and the documentation processes were not there as a foundation. When we look at libraries in a historic perspective, at Naudés' opening of the world's first public libraries, at the public libraries of dawning democracies, or at the digital libraries in contemporary universities, it is the ability to use professional skills to collect, organize, and provide

---

12. Joacim Hansson, "Documentality and Legitimacy in Future Libraries: An Analytical Framework for Initiated Speculation," *New Library World* 116, no. 1/2 (2015): 4-14.

access to the right kind of document in every specific situation that is the common ground. All the other activities have their meanings too, but when creating an intellectual bedrock for an emancipatory agenda in librarianship by developing a relevant Library and Information Science education, then shifting discourses from information to documentation must be seen as desirable. And, as noted before, such a shift has already been prepared for in the current educational discourse through the inability of the iSchool movement to define its most central concept—information—as anything other than a socially constructed document. This argument of course run the risk of over-simplification. Clearly, it does not suffice to exchange information for documentation on all levels, but having it as the basis for discussion is possible. And, in terms of encouraging students of librarianship and their ability to create a professional identity during their years at university, a shift in discourse would have a significant impact. A *dSchool movement*—why not?

## *Maintaining a Home in the Humanities*

The most common placement of Library and Information Science in universities is at the intersection between the social sciences and the humanities. This is not a static position—because the information science part of the discipline has an increased tendency to lean towards computer science and informatics, the emphasis of the discipline has become balanced towards the technological side as well. This complexity is important to address in direct relation to librarianship as it governs what attitudes and ideals students internalize during their work to become librarians. Technology is an important factor in librarianship. The shift in academic library practice due to the digitization of scholarly publishing, the growing field of data curation, and the belief that open access to scientific results is for the greater good places it in the middle of these developments in a way which, I would argue, has been to the benefit of the profession. Academic librarians today have a strong position in their universities. Once again, the situation is more complex when turning towards the realm of public libraries. A major feature in the information science discourse, as well as in defining the iSchool movement, is decontextualization. Reliance on information technology obscures the local aspects of librarianship. In doing this, the technological paradigm reduces the impetus of critical thought, as the focus is strongly set on practical solutions and immediate implementation. In order to fulfill the democratic mission of public librarianship and the inherent emancipatory character of the library institution as such, local perspectives and practices must be made prominent and promoted through education. It is here that we see the real struggle between the perspectives highlighted by the Panda Syndrome studies which I referred to earlier. The ideal of a locally grounded practice, relating to values and ideals of the profession as they have developed in relation to social and cultural conditions over time, is set against a more technology-driven ideal in which librarians are defined as information workers and part of the capitalist logic of the information industry. The result in local communities is a variety of conceptions of the library, from it being a center for technology and entertainment to it being a center for local engagement and cultural diversity, a center for the promotion of reading and cultural identity. Of course, this binary opposition is for the sake of argument—in reality there is no reason why both perspectives should not be able to complement each other and usually they do. It does, however, matter when looking at the ideals of library education. Higher education rarely promotes the connection between the local and the emancipatory. The ideal of entrepreneurialism that permeates all aspects of most European universities has its target set on creating a useful workforce for accelerated economic growth, without concern for the social distribution of wealth, based on a belief in "knowledge" as a key product. But how does this product ship from the universities and get out into the marketplace?

We are time and again reminded that for the large international social media corporations, users are not really the customers but rather the products, offered to other companies that benefit from the private data we so happily put at their disposal. It is very much the same with today's universities. In literature critical of recent developments in contemporary higher education, the idea that students are seen, not least by themselves, as customers is common. It is time to revise that notion and instead start to talk of students as the products of universities, delivered to the market on graduation day to customers, in the capacity of their newly gained employability. The competitive "knowledge" that universities claim to deliver to both the private and public sector is no longer primarily bound in other product segments such as scientific publications—it is bound in the acquired entrepreneurial mindset of the students themselves. Just as technology relates to a certain kind of universalism, based on the logic of capitalism and devoid of any values other than those of speed and money, so do universities today reproduce a similar kind of reductionistic universalism. A different kind of universal ideal is found in the humanities, and the debate on how to maintain that in future higher education is as patient as it is defiant. In the face of drastic cuts in the humanities, so ubiquitous in countries with higher education afflicted by neoliberal ideals, Martha Nussbaum has created a manifesto, *Not for Profit: Why Democracy Needs the Humanities*, which is refreshingly straightforward;

> [e]ducators for economic growth will do more than ignore the arts. They will fear them. For a cultivated and developed sympathy is a particularly dangerous enemy of obtuseness, and moral obtuseness is necessary to carry out programs of economic development that ignore inequality. It is easier to treat people as objects to be manipulated if you have never learned any other way to see them.[13]

She emphasizes that universities which prioritize their contributions to economic growth not only tend to disregard various forms of Socratic pedagogics, encouragement of critical thinking, and development of empathy in the students' view of the world, they work directly against democracy as such. There is, as it happens, no connection between economic growth and democratic development, gender equality, diversity, freedom of expression, and other human rights—something humanity has learned the hard way from the thriving economies of apartheid South Africa, the repressive political system of China and, indeed, the neo-nationalist USA of today. Instead, insistence on civility, empathy, and critical analysis tends to be seen as an obstacle to the docility required from students and workers in the technocentric neoliberal system of learning.

Nussbaum does not only defend the liberal arts system in American universities, she suggest a whole new paradigm for learning: "the human development paradigm."[14] "The

---

13. Martha C. Nussbaum, *Not for Profit: Why Democracy Needs the Humanities* (Princeton, NJ: Princeton University Press, 2010), 23.

14. Nussbaum, 24-26.

Human Development model," she writes, "is committed to democracy, since having a voice in the choice of the policies that govern one's life is a key ingredient in a life worthy of human dignity."[15] But, the model also commits to the arts and the need for imagination and artistic expression as a means to reach the other, not as an adversary but as an equal. The other individual is seen as an end, not as a means, for entrepreneurial exchange. The liberal arts model has been exported to European countries with various degrees of success, but has never really "made it" into the general consciousness of European higher education. This has created a situation for the humanities which is even more problematic than the one described by Nussbaum. The marginalization of the humanities tends to become more invisible if no fundamental status is granted them in the first place, and their defense tends to take other directions, mostly far less radical than the one presented by Nussbaum.

More often the defense of the humanities is to be formulated as a concern over how they can be adapted and applied in a system that clearly does not know what to do with them. Attacks from industry representatives and organizations imply that universities should refrain from offering courses on the world of Harry Potter or the films of Ingmar Bergman, lumping the humanities under the label "hobby courses" not worthy of public funding. These attacks are met by passive-aggressive attempts to argue for the value of such courses for people in business as well. What then does all of this has to do with librarianship and library education?

In discussing issues critical to academia, few have come as close as Martha Nussbaum to the emancipatory ethos of

---

15. Nussbaum, 24.

librarianship that I discussed in chapter 2. Her formulation of the Human Development Paradigm could easily be translated into a paradigm for librarianship that would go hand in hand with Axel Honneth's ideas of individual, social, and legal recognition of the other as a prerequisite for a society driven by civility—and it resonates well with library practice as such. Her pedagogical formulations through Socratic argumentation and the connection between thought and practical life in line with the ideals of John Dewey resonate well with the critical pedagogics developed in librarianship as initiated by James Elmborg and continued by Annie Downey and others today.[16] It easily relates to the critical perspectives on subject analysis, classification, and the practice of ordering document collections as formulated by scholars such as Hope Olson and Melissa Adler.[17] This research mirrors library ideals, challenges established patriarchal hierarchies, creates a bedrock for emancipatory practice development, and is in turn fueled by just that. Library and Information Science and librarianship are at their most fruitful when research and professional practice can find a common direction in which to lead discourse. The result becomes, to once again borrow a formulation from Nussbaum in her discussion on democratic education, "not a cultivated gentleman, stuffed with the wisdom of the ages, but an active, critical, reflective,

---

16. James Elmborg, "Critical Information Literacy: Implication for Instructional Practice," *Journal of Academic Librarianship* 23, no. 2 (2006): 192-199; Annie Downey, *Critical Information Literacy: Foundations, Inspiration, Ideas* (Sacramento, CA: Library Juice Press, 2016).

17. Hope Olson, *The Power to Name: Locating the Limits of Subject Representation in Libraries* (Dordrecht: Kluwer, 2002); Melissa Adler, *Cruising the Library: Perversities in the Organization of Knowledge* (New York: Fordham University Press, 2017).

and empathetic member of a community of equals, capable of exchanging ideas on the basis of respect and understanding with people from many different backgrounds."[18] This is the emblematic librarian.

Michael Buckland has drawn attention to the liberal arts concept in a somewhat different but equally challenging manner, trying out the thought of Library and Information Science as a liberal arts construct in itself. This idea was presented at the second CoLIS conference in 1996, suggesting that if a university should decide to follow through on adjusting to the trope of the information society, then why not let Library and Information Science provide part of the *Bildung* needed in preparation for more specialized study? In such an argument, it is assumed that the courses taught within Library and Information Science are so in line with the general knowledge needed to live and develop as a civilized human being in the information society that the topics that constitute the discipline could be studied for their own sake. This would also rewrite the position of the discipline in its role as preparation for work in professional librarianship. Buckland concludes:

> The real reason not to create a liberal arts department of LIS is not that it is not a good idea in itself, but that there is an even more powerful option at hand; a conception of LIS in which professional education in LIS is positioned *within* a liberal arts conception of LIS. Here one could combine all the advantages of both.[19]

---

18. Nussbaum, *Not for Profit*, 141.

19. Michael Buckland, "The 'Liberal Arts' of Library and Information Science and the Research University Environment," in *Information Science: Integration in Perspective: Proceedings of the 2nd International Conference on Conceptions of Library and Information Science, Copenhagen, October 13-16, 1996*, eds. Peter

Buckland never further pursued this idea, nor did anybody else to the best of my knowledge. But perhaps it is there already, albeit in a slightly different form, with the academic librarians who practice critical instruction while teaching information literacy on a daily basis to students in all disciplines and at all levels in our universities. Still, one must ask: would a strengthened liberal arts system in Europe benefit from the inclusion of Library and Information Science, and would Library and Information Science benefit from being part of the liberal arts construct as we see it today in the USA? If so, Library and Information Science would need to be defined as a fundamentally humanistic field of research and study. This does not necessarily stand in opposition to traditional Library and Information Science programs, which focus on providing the intellectual platform for professional library practice. Instead it is in line with the discipline's present position in many schools in Europe, not least in the Scandinavian countries, and is also something which resonates in relation to the defense of the humanities as formulated by Nussbaum. Much of what she writes about was once an integral part of the popular adult education system that developed in parallel with the more formalized public school structure in the early phases of the development of the welfare states of Sweden, Denmark, and Norway.[20] This parallel educational system was driven by an explicitly emancipatory agenda, and it is from the collections in schools and libraries of the Good Templar movement and workers'

---

Ingwersen and Niels Ole Pors (Copenhagen: Royal School of Librarianship, 1996b), 83. Italics in original.

20. The Swedish term for this kind of popular adult education is *folkbildning*, which literally means "*Bildung* for the people."

associations that Scandinavian public libraries are built. If this tells us anything it is this: the connection between Socratic, emancipatory pedagogics, the cultivation of imagination and civility, and the practice of librarianship is such that Library and Information Science here finds its strongest form of legitimacy. Treating Library and Information Science as a discipline within the humanities provides for perspectives in direct opposition to contemporary educational ideals, placing the independent, creative, and empathetic human being at the center of interest—this is also what librarians do in their daily efforts to maintain the universality of being human. It is, basically, a bond of loyalty in equal parts demanding and invigorating.

## *Ethos Resurrected—Towards an Emancipatory Narrative of Librarianship Education*

Pushing Library and Information Science in a direction towards the study of documents and documentation processes while maintaining a firmly humanist perspective brings education for librarianship closer to its core. It is important to never lose sight of the fact that librarianship is a profession driven by the cultural and the social, not the technological—and no, these are not one and the same. Such redirection should not be done for sentimental purposes, but rather is necessary in order to meet demands from the profession's increasingly complex environments. New Public Management governance is built on de-professionalization and a transfer of organizational power away from professionals (physicians, teachers, librarians) towards an ever-growing administrative body engaged in evaluation, ranking of measured outcomes, and branding of the professional's activities. This ideological practice is not to the benefit of higher education, nor of librarianship, and there is thus good reason to resist it and find ways to maintain the moral ground of both scholarly work and librarianship—and the connections between the two. Indeed, the suggestion to define Library and Information Science as part of the humanities is motivated by reasons that are fundamentally moral and ethical. I have in this essay portrayed higher education as "lost" to the neoliberal agenda, and libraries as still motivated by a guiding ethos. While university leaders have given up on any fundamental ideal of the university, whether you retract it from Wilhelm von Humboldt's motto *Einsamkeit und Freiheit* or John Henry Newman's more socially-oriented ideals, librarians have maintained the ability to relate their institutions to a fundamental notion of commonsense, which has been protecting them from the moral and ethical erosion brought on by the hegemonic rules of governance in the past.

When educating librarians, it is key that Library and Information Science scholars devote both research and undergraduate education to the persistent ideals of librarianship. These are the ideals that ought to be the subject of their loyalty—not the whims of entrepreneurialism in their departments, schools, and faculties. Of course, this is easier said than done, partly because all problems dealt with in Library and Information Science research do not explicitly relate to practical librarianship, nor should they. Most of them are, however, possible to relate to the professional and institutional practices which provide the fundamental legitimacy of the discipline. If not, they are probably better dealt with somewhere else. In order to create an intellectual environment which can prepare students for work in various types of libraries, scholars in Library and Information Science departments must themselves create an environment based on open thought, critical enquiry, and a persistent ethos.

Connecting education in librarianship to a professional core of ethical essentials may be seen as somewhat conservative, and proponents of such suggestions have from time to time been accused of being traditionalists and feeding inertia in relation to a primarily technological development with which libraries need to keep up-to-speed. I claim that today, in a political environment that explicitly deconstructs institutional and professional values, maintaining them is well in line with a radical agenda for achieving emancipatory resilience. It is, however, not self-evident how to define such a core. Wallace Koehler, in his *Ethics and Values in Librarianship: A History*, defines the core values of librarianship in no less than thirty paragraphs, summing up suggestions from both tradition and contemporary debate.[21] Perhaps more well-known are the eight "enduring values" suggested by Michael Gorman in 2000:[22]

- Stewardship
- Service
- Intellectual freedom
- Rationalism
- Literacy and learning
- Equity of access to recorded knowledge and information
- Privacy
- Democracy

---

21. Wallace Koehler, *Ethics and Values in Librarianship: A History* (Lanham, MD: Rowman & Littlefield, 2015), 25.

22. Gorman, *Our Enduring Values*, 26-27.

Looking at history, these themes represent discourses that undoubtedly have formed a basis for a resilient ethos in the practice of professional librarianship. They have also in many ways come to be seen as synonymous with the library institution as well, regardless of whether we are considering a small rural public library or a large university library. In relation to the suggestion here to decrease the influence of the information discourse in favor of a more document-oriented one, I would especially point to the question of recorded knowledge, without which a library simply does not exist. From this basis forward, it becomes possible to extend into becoming low-intensive meeting places, developing practices for instruction and pedagogics, setting up maker-spaces, and doing the other things that are parts of the daily work of librarians. The responsibility of Library and Information Science in relation to this ethos is to raise an awareness among students as to what challenges will come in their future practice and how to claim and use this ethos, not just as a toolbox but as a marker of identity—"this is who we are and this is what we do." There are at least four ways in which educators may deal with ethics in programs of Library and Information Science:

- By showing how to create a direction when ethical dilemmas appear. This is not least relevant in relation to the neoliberal concept of "userism."
- By learning how to question and counteract interests of the institution and of professional practice that are not benevolent—be they political, economic, technological, or managerial.
- By building a sense of meaningfulness. Knowing the ethos of the profession develops a sense of right and

wrong that is used in upholding integrity in daily practice. This in turn leads to increased wellbeing and an ability to resist demands such as unreflected innovation and decision-making.
- By analyzing and debating relevant legislation framing the institutional aspects of libraries. The function libraries are given in a specific country or region through legislation and public policies contributes to the definition of the librarian's role. A strong legislative foundation is a good tool to have, but it must always be kept alive.

For the emancipatory character of librarianship to develop from the basis of educational programs and other efforts, we need to embrace the conflictual character of democracy by formulating fundamental patterns of power relevant for the sector. Whether working in libraries with critical information literacy or within a critical knowledge organization, one question must permeate all activities: who benefits? The recognition of librarianship as not just a welfare profession but also an emancipatory one is based on the ability to identify basic patterns of power. In whose interests the work is being done is the foremost question that must be put at the center, and the answer must always be those who in each situation can be defined as underprivileged—be it the young university student trying to make sense of the jungle of scholarly publishing, the elderly woman who wants to understand the internet, the newly arrived war-traumatized refugee, the homeless man sheltering from the winter cold, or the little child in the midst of her insecure quest for conquering a language through reading. The contemporary university does not have room for conflict, nor does the information industry, but it is necessary to persevere. If for nothing else, it must be done for the survival of the professional librarian: unafraid and guided by a strong ethos in the midst of the ever-expanding pluriverse of documents and documentation processes, a librarian with an identity built on the solid foundation of a relevant education in Library and Information Science.

# References

Adler, Melissa. *Cruising the Library: Perversities in the Organization of Knowledge*. New York: Fordham University Press, 2017.

*En akademi i tiden—ökad frihet för universitet och högskolor*. Regeringens proposition 2009/10:149. https://www.regeringen.se/contentassets/07a972fdbfdd43789da5a5b03dbb6f4a/en-akademi-i-tiden---okad-frihet-for-universitet-och-hogskolor-prop.-200910149.

Andersen, Jack, Ragnar Andreas Audunson, Svanhild Aabø, Helena Francke, Henrik Jochumsen, and Michael Kristiansson. "Partnership with Society: A Social and Cultural Approach to iSchool-Research. *Proceedings, iConference 2016*, Philadelphia, PA, 2016. https://www.ideals.illinois.edu/bitstream/handle/2142/89445/Andersen496.pdf.

Anderson, Joel. "Situating Axel Honneth in the Frankfurt School Tradition." In *Axel Honneth: Critical Essays. With a Reply by Axel Honneth*, edited by Danielle Petherbridge, 31-57. Leiden: Brill, 2011.

Audunson, Ragnar. "The Public Library as a Meeting Place in a Multicultural and Digital Context: The Necessity of Low-Intensive Meeting-Places." *Journal of Documentation* 61, no. 3 (2005): 429-441.

Audunson, Ragnar, and Liv Gjestrum. "Bibliotek- og informasjonsfaglig utdanning: Fra etatsskole til iSchool." In *Samle, formidle, dele: 75 år med bibliotekarutdanning*, edited by Ragnar Andreas Audunson, 11-46. Oslo: ABM-Media AS, 2015.

Bawden, David. "Information and Digital Literacies: A Review of Concepts." *Journal of Documentation* 57, no. 2 (2001): 218-259.

Benoit, Gerald. "Critical Theory and the Legitimation of Library and Information Science." *Information Research* 12 no. 4 (2007): paper colis30: http://InformationR.net/ir/12-4/colis30.html.

Berg, Maggie, and Barbara K. Seeber. *The Slow Professor: Challenging the Culture of Speed in the Academy*. Toronto: University of Toronto Press, 2016.

Bishop, Clair. *Artificial Hells: Participatory Art and the Politics of Spectatorship*. London: Verso, 2012.

Blomberg, Barbro, and Göran Widebäck, eds.. *Biblioteket som serviceföretag: kunden i centrum*. Stockholm: Forskningsrådsnämnden, 1992.

*Bologna Declaration of 19 June 1999: Joint Declaration of the European ministers of education*. https://www.eurashe.eu/library/modernising-phe/Bologna_1999_Bologna-Declaration.pdf.

Bonnici, Laurie J., Manimegalai M. Subramaniam, and Kathleen Burnett. "Everything Old is New Again: The Evolution of Library and Information Science

Education from LIS to iField." *Journal of Education for Library and Information Science* 50, no. 4 (2009): 263-274.

Borup Larsen, Jeannie. "A survey of Library and Information Schools in Europe." In *European curriculum reflections on Library and Information Science education*, edited by Leif Kajberg and Leif Lorring, 232-241. Copenhagen: Royal School of Library and Information Science, 2005. https://www.asis.org/Bulletin/Dec-06/EuropeanLIS.pdf.

Bourriaud, Nicholas. *Relational Aesthetics*. Paris: Les Presses du Réel, 1998.

Briet, Suzanne. *What is Documentation? English Translation of the Classic French Text*, translated and edited by Ronald E. Day and Laurent Martinet. Lanham, MD: Scarecrow Press 1951/2006.

Bruce, Harry. "The Audacious Vision of Information Schools." *Journal of Library and Information Science* 37, no. 1 (2011): 4-10.

Buckland, Michael. "Documentation, Information Science, and Library Science in the USA." *Information Processing and Management* 32, no. 1 (1996): 63-76.

———. "The 'Liberal Arts' of Library and Information Science and the Research University Environment." In *Information Science: Integration in Perspective: Proceedings of the 2nd International Conference on Conceptions of Library and Information Science, Copenhagen, October 13-16, 1996*, edited by Peter

Ingwersen and Niels Ole Pors, 75-84. Copenhagen: Royal School of Librarianship, 1996.

———. "What is a Document?" *Journal of the American Society for Information Science* 48, no. 9 (1997): 804-809.

———. "Information Schools: A Monk, Library Science and the Information Age." *Bibliothekswissenschaft—quo vadis? Eine Disziplin zweischen Traditionen und Visionen: Programme, Modelle, Forschungsaufgaben / Library Science—quo vadis? A Discipline between Challenges and Opportunities: Programs, Models, Research Assignments*, 19-32. München: K. G. Saur, 2005.

———. "What Kind of Science *Can* Information Science Be?" *Journal of the American Society for Information Science and Technology* 63, no. 1 (2012): 1-7.

Budd, John M., and Catherine Dumas. "Epistemic Multiplicity in iSchools: Expanding Knowledge through Interdisciplinarity / La multiplicité épistémic dans les iSchools: le developpement des connaissances grâce à l'interdisciplinarité." *Canadian Journal of Information and Library Science* 38, no. 4 (2014): 271-286.

Buschman, John. *Dismantling the Public Sphere: Situating and Sustaining Librarianship in the Age of the New Public Philosophy*. Westport, CT: Libraries Unlimited, 2003.

———. "Democratic Theory in Library and Information Science: Toward an Emendation." *Journal of the American Association for Information Science and Technology* 58, no. 10 (2007):1483-1496.

———. "The Social as Fundamental and a Source of the Critical: Jürgen Habermas." In *Critical theory for Library and Information Science: Exploring the Social from across the Disciplines*, edited by Gloria J. Leckie, Lisa M. Given, and John E. Buschman, 161-172. Santa Barbara, CA: Libraries Unlimited, 2010.

Carruthers, Alexandra. "Social Reproduction in the Early American Public Library: Exploring the Connections between Capital and Gender." In *Class and Librarianship: Essays at the Intersection of Information, Labor and Capital*, edited by Erik Estep and Nathaniel Enright, 25-48. Sacramento, CA: Library Juice Press, 2016.

Casson, Lionel. *Libraries in the Ancient World*. New Haven, CT: Yale University Press, 2001.

Chang, Lulu. "Google Eliminated That 'Don't be Evil' Motto." *Digital Trends,* 21 May 2018. https://www.digitaltrends.com/computing/google-dont-be-evil/.

Chu, Heting. "iSchools and Non-iSchools in the USA: An Examination of Their Master's Programs." *Education for Information* 29 (2012): 1-17.

Clement, Claude. *Musei sive Bibliothecae tam privatae quàm publicae Extructio, Instructio, Cura, Usus. Libri IV. Accessit accurata descriptio Regiae Bibliothecae S.*

> *Laurentii Escurialis: Insuper Paraenesis allegorica ad maorem literarum. Opus multiplici eruditione sacra simul et humana refertum; praeceptis moralibus et literariis, architecturae et picturae subiectionibus, inscriptionibus et Emblematis, antiquitatis philogicae monumentis, atque oratoriis schematis utiliter et amoenè tesséllatum.* Lyon, 1635.

Cope, Jonathan T. "The Reconquista Student: Critical Information Literacy, Civics, and Confronting Student Intolerance." *Communications in Information Literacy* 11, no. 2 (2017): 264-282.

Cosette, André. *Humanism and Libraries: An Essay on the Philosophy of Librarianship*. Duluth, MN: Library Juice Press, 1976/2009.

Dahler-Larsen, Peter. "The New Configuration of Metrics, Rules, and Guidelines Creates a Disturbing Ambiguity in Academia." *LSE Impact Blog*, July 13th 2017. http://blogs.lse.ac.uk/impactofsocialsciences/2017/07/13/the-new-configuration-of-metrics-rules-and-guidelines-creates-a-disturbing-ambiguity-in-academia/.

Day, Ronald E. "Tropes, History and Ethics in Professional Discourse and Information Science." *Journal of the American Society for Information Science* 51, no. 5 (2000): 469-475.

———. *The Modern Invention of Information: Discourse, History and Power*. Carbondale, IL: Southern Illinois University Press, 2001.

*Demokratins skattkammare: förslag till en nationella biblioteksstrategi*. Stockholm: Kungliga biblioteket, 2019.

Dervin, Brenda. "Information <–> Democracy: An Examination of Underlying Assumptions." *Journal of the American Society for Information Science* 45, no. 6 (1994): 369-385.

———. "Given a Context by Another Name: Methodological Tools for Taming the Unruly Beast." In *Information Seeking in Context: Proceedings of an International Conference on Research in Information Needs, Seeking and Use in Different Contexts, 14-16 August, Tampere, Finland*, edited by Pertti Vakkari, Reijo Savolainen, and Brenda Dervin, 13-38. London: Taylor Graham, 1996.

Downey, Annie. *Critical Information Literacy: Foundations, Inspiration, Ideas*. Sacramento, CA: Library Juice Press, 2016.

Edmundson, Mark. "Under the Sign of Satan: William Blake in the Corporate University." T*he Hedgehog Review* 14, no. 1 (2012). http://iasc-culture.org/THR/THR_article_2012_Spring_Edmundson.php.

Elmborg, James. "Critical Information Literacy: Implication for Instructional Practice." *Journal of Academic Librarianship* 23, no. 2 (2006): 192-199.

Emilsson, Aron, Angelika Bengtsson, Sara-Lena Bjälkö, and Cassandra Sundin. *Biblioteksfrågor*. Motion till riksdagen 2016/17 2208.

European Commission. Horizon 2020. https://ec.europa.eu/programmes/horizon2020/en.

European Commission. Horizon 2020, Social Sciences and Humanities. https://ec.europa.eu/programmes/horizon2020/en/area/social-sciences-and-humanities.

Ferraris, Maurizio. *Documentality: Why It is Necessary to Leave Traces*. New York: Fordham University Press, 2013.

Floridi, Luciano. *The 4th Revolution: How the Infosphere is Reshaping Human Reality*. Oxford, UK: Oxford University Press, 2014.

Friberg, Torbjörn. "Akademiska subjekt och politisk-ekonomiska processer." In *Den högre utbildningen: ett fält av marknad och politik*, edited by Daniel Ankaroo and Torbjörn Friberg, 101-126. Möklinta: Gidlunds, 2012.

Frohmann, Bernd. "The Power of Images: A Discourse Analysis of the Cognitive Viewpoint." *Journal of Documentation* 48, no. 4 (1992): 365-386.

———. *Deflating Information: From Science Studies to Documentation*. Toronto: Toronto University Press, 2004.

Furner, Jonathan. "Information Studies without Information." *Library Trends* 52, no. 3 (2004): 427-446.

Giddens, Anthony. *The Third Way: The Renewal of Social Democracy*. Cambridge, UK: Polity Press, 1998.

———. *The Third Way and Its Critics*. Cambridge, UK: Polity Press, 2000.

Ginsberg, Benjamin. *The Fall of the Faculty: The Rise of the All-Administrative University and Why It Matters*. Oxford, UK: Oxford University Press, 2011.

Golub, Koraljka, Joacim Hansson, and Lars Seldén. "Cult of the 'I': Organizational Symbolism and Curricula in Three Scandinavian iSchools with Comparisons to Three American." *Journal of Documentation* 73, no. 1 (2017): 48-74.

Goodman, Paul. *Growing Up Absurd: Problems of Youth in the Organized Society*. New York: New York Review Books, 1960/2012.

Gorman, Michael. *Our Enduring Values: Librarianship in the 21st Century*. Chicago: American Library Association, 2000.

*A Guiding Framework for Entrepreneurial Universities*. European Commission / OECD, 2012. https://www.oecd.org/site/cfecpr/EC-OECD%20Entrepreneurial%20Universities%20Framework.pdf

Habermas, Jürgen. *The Theory of Communicative Action, Volume 1: Reason and the Rationalization of Society*. London: Heinemann, 1984.

Hammarfelt, Björn, Sarah de Rijcke, and Alexander D. Rushforth. "Quantified Academic Selves: The Gamification of Research through Social Networking Services." *Information Research* 21, no. 2 (2016):

Paper SM1. http://www.informationr.net/ir/21-2/SM1.html#.Wxo12oa-nBI.

Hansson, Joacim "The Social Legitimacy of Library and Information Science: Reconsidering the Institutional Paradigm." In *Aware and Responsible: Papers of the Nordic-International Colloquium on Social and Cultural Awareness and Responsibility in Library, Information and Documentation Studies (SCARLID)*, edited by W. Boyd Rayward, 49-69. Lanham, MD: Scarecrow Press, 2004.

———. "Chantal Mouffe's Theory of Agonistic Pluralism and Its Relevance for Library and Information Science Research." In *Critical Theory for Library and Information Science: Exploring the Social from Across the Disciplines*, edited by Gloria J. Leckie, Lisa M. Given, and John E. Buschman, 249-257. Santa Barbara, CA: Libraries Unlimited, 2010.

———. "Documentality and Legitimacy in Future Libraries: An Analytical Framework for Initiated Speculation." *New Library World* 116, no. 1/2 (2015): 4-14.

Hansson, Joacim, Åse Hedemark, Ulrika Kjellman, Jenny Lindberg, Jan Nolin, Olof Sundin, and Per Wisselgren. *Profession, utbildning forskning: biblioteks- och informationsvetenskap för en stärkt bibliotekarieprofession*. Stockholm: Kungliga Biblioteket, 2018.

Hauptman, Robert. *Ethics and Librarianship*. Jefferson, NC: McFarland, 2002.

Hjørland, Birger. "Library and Information Science: Practice, Theory, and Philosophical Basis." *Information Processing and Management* 36 (2000): 501-531.

Honneth, Axel. *The Struggle for Recognition: The Moral Grammar of Social Conflicts*. Cambridge, UK: Polity Press, 1995.

Honoré, Carl. *In Praise of Slowness: Challenging the Cult of Speed*. New York: Harper Collins, 2005.

Ibekwe-SanJuan, Fidelia. *La science de l'information: origines, théories et paradigmes*, Paris: Lavoisier, 2012.

Ingwersen, Peter, and Niels Ole Pors, eds. *Information Science: Integration in Perspective: Proceedings of the Second International Conference on Conceptions of Library and Information Science, October 13-16, 1996, Copenhagen, Denmark*. Copenhagen: The Royal School of Librarianship, 1996.

Ingraham, Christopher. "An Awful Lot of People Use and Love Their Public Library, as an Economics Professor Discovered this Weekend." *Washington Post*, July 23, 2018. https://www.washingtonpost.com/business/2018/07/23/an-awful-lot-people-use-love-their-public-library-an-economics-professor-discovered-this-weekend.

Ingwersen, Peter, and Järvelin, Kalervo. *The Turn: Integration of Information Seeking and Retrieval in Context*. Dordrecht: Springer, 2005.

Johannsen, Carl Gustav. *Staff-Less Libraries: Innovative Staff Design*. Oxford, UK: Chandos, 2017.

Kann-Christensen, Nanna, and Jack Andersen "Developing the Library: Between Efficiency, Accountability, and Forms of Recognition." *Journal of Documentation* 65, no. 2 (2009): 208-222.

Karlsohn, Thomas. *Universitetets idé: sexton nyckeltexter*. Göteborg: Daidalos, 2016.

Kjorstad, Monica, and Maj-Britt Solem. *Critical Realism for Welfare Professions*. London: Routledge, 2018.

Koehler, Wallace. *Ethics and Values in Librarianship: A History*. Lanham, MD: Rowman & Littlefield, 2015.

Finlex. Lag om allmänna bibliotek, 29.12.2016/1492. https://www.finlex.fi/sv/laki/ajantasa/2016/20161492

Larson, Magali Sarfatti. *The Rise of Professionalism: Monopolies of Competence and Sheltered Markets*. New Brunswick, Canada: Transaction Pub., 2013.

Lash, Scott. *Critique of Information*. London: Sage, 2002.

Levy, David M. *Scrolling Forward: Making Sense of Documents in the Digital Age*. New York: Arcade Publishing, 2001.

Linnaeus University. "The Entrepreneurial University." June 16, 2016. https://lnu.se/en/meet-linnaeus-university/This-is-linnaeus-university/vision-and-basic-principles/the-entrepreneurial-university/.

Lloyd, Annemaree. "Researching Fractured (Information) Landscapes: Implications for Library and Information Science Researchers Undertaking Research with Refugees and Forced Migration Studies." *Journal of Documentation 73*, no. 1 (2017): 1-15.

Lovdata. Lov om Folkebibliotek. https://lovdata.no/dokument/NL/lov/1985-12-20-108#KAPITTEL_1.

Lynch, Beverly P. "Library Education: Its Past, Its Present, Its Future." *Library Trends* 56, no. 4 (2008): 931-953.

Observatory. *Magna Charta Universitatem*. Bologna, 1988. http://www.magna-charta.org/magna-charta-universitatum/the-magna-charta-1.

Marinetti, Filippo Tommasso. *The Founding and Manifesto of Futurism*. London: Art Press Books, 2016.

Marx, Karl, and Friedrich Engels. *The Communist Manifesto*. London: Penguin, 1848/2015.

Masson, André, and Denis Pallier. *Les bibliothèques*, Paris: Presses Universitaires de France, 1961.

Mouffe, Chantal. *The Democratic Paradox*. London: Verso, 2000.

———. *On the Political*. Abingdon, UK: Routledge, 2005.

Mourdoukoutas, Panos. "Amazon Should Replace Local Libraries to Save Taxpayers Money." *Forbes*, July 21 2018. http://archive.is/mPceN.

Muddiman, Dave, Shiraz Durani, John Pateman, Martin Dutch, Rebecca Linley, and John Vincent. "Open to All? The Public Library and Social Exclusion: Executive Summary. *New Library World* 102, no. 4/5 (2001): 154-158.

Mycue, David. "Founder of the Vatican Library: Nicholas V or Sixtus IV?" *Journal of Library History* 16, no. 1(1981): 121-133.

Naudé, Gabriel. *Advis pour dresser une bibliothèque: reproduction de l'édition de 1644 précédée de L'Advis, manifeste de la bibliothèque érudite par Claude Jolly, directeur de la bibliothèque de la Sorbonne.* Paris: Klinksieck, 1644/1994.

Nicholson, Karen P., and Maura Seale, eds. *The Politics of Theory and the Practice of Critical Librarianship.* Sacramento, CA: Library Juice Press, 2018.

Nolin, Jan. *In Search of a New Theory of Professions.* Borås: Högskolan i Borås, 2008.

Nolin, Jan, and Fredrik Åström. "Turning Weakness into Strength: Strategies for Future LIS." *Journal of Documentation* 66, no. 1 (2010): 7-27.

Nussbaum, Martha C. *Not for Profit: Why Democracy Needs the Humanities.* Princeton, NJ: Princeton University Press, 2010.

Olson, Hope. *The Power to Name: Locating the Limits of Subject Representation in Libraries.* Dordrecht: Kluwer, 2002.

O'Neill, Maggie. "The Slow University: Work, Time and Well-Being." *Forum: Qualitative Social Research / Sozialforschung* 15, no. 3 (2014): Art. 14.

Rayward, W. Boyd. "The Origins of Information Science and the International Institute of Bibliography/ International Federation for Information and Documentation (FID)." *Journal of the American Society for Information Science* 48, no. 4 (1997): 289-300.

Regneala, Mircea. "An Overview of Contemporary Librarianship Education." *Studii de biblioteconomie si stiinta informarii / Library and Information Science Research*, No. 9/2005-10/2006 (2006): 16-22.

Rivano Eckerdal, Johanna. "Libraries, Democracy, Information, and Citizenship: An Agonistic Reading of Central Library and Information Studies' Concepts." *Journal of Documentation* 73, no. 5 (2017): 1010-1033.

Rosa, Hartmut. *Social Acceleration: A New Theory of Modernity*. New York: Columbia University Press, 2015.

Rovelstad, Mathilde V. "Two Seventeenth Century Library Handbooks: Two Different Library Theories." *Libraries and Culture* 35 no. 4 (2000): 540-556.

Schrettinger, Marti. *Handbuch der Bibliothek-Wissenshaft besonders zum gebrauche für Nicht-Bibliotekthekare, welche ihre Privat-Büchersammlungen selbst einrichten wollen*. Wien, 1834. Digitized version available for download at Bayerische Staatsbibliothek, catalog post: Rar. 723, Urn:nbn:de:bvb:12-bsb10858302-8.

Seadle, Michael, and Elke Greifeneder. "Envisioning an iSchool Curriculum." *Information Research* 12, no. 4 (2007): paper colise02.

Seale, Maura. "The Neoliberal Library." In *Information Literacy and Social Justice: Radical Professional Practice*, edited by Lua Gregory and Shana Higgins, 39-61, Sacramento, CA: Library Juice Press, 2013.

Shannon, Claude, and Warren Weaver. *The Mathematical Theory of Communication*. Urbana, IL: University of Illinois Press, 1963.

Smelser, Neil J. *Dynamics of the Contemporary University: Growth, Accretion, and Conflict*. Berkeley, CA: University of California Press, 2013.

*Sorbonne Joint Declaration: Joint Declaration on the Harmonisation of the Architecture of the European Higher Education System, Paris, the Sorbonne 25 May 1998*. http://media.ehea.info/file/1998_Sorbonne/61/2/1998_Sorbonne_Declaration_English_552612.pdf.

Sperrer, Martin, Christina Müller, and Julia Soos. "The Concept of the Entrepreneurial University Applied to Universities of Technology in Austria: Already Reality or Visions of the Future?" *Technology Innovation Management Review* 6, no. 10 (2016): 37-44.

Suominen, Vesa. *About and on Behalf of* Sriptum Est: *The Literary, Bibliographic and Educational Rationality* sui generis *of the Library and Librarianship on the Top of What Literature has Produced*. Oulu: University of Oulu, 2016.

Sutton, Stuart A. "The Panda Syndrome II: Innovation, Discontinuous Change and LIS Education." *Journal of Education for Library and Information Science* 40, no. 4 (1999): 247-262.

Svensk författningssamling 1974:152. http://www.riksdagen.se/sv/dokument-lagar/dokument/svensk-forfattningssamling/kungorelse-1974152-om-beslutad-ny-regeringsform_sfs-1974-152.

Swedish Research Council. *Research Project Grant for Digitisation and Accessibility of Cultural Heritage Collections.* 22 May 2018. https://vr.se/english/calls-and-decisions/calls/calls/2018-06-05-research-project-grant-for-digitisation-and-accessibility-of-cultural-heritage-collections.html.

Toffler, Alvin. *The Third Wave*. New York: Bantam, 1980.

Vakkari, Pertti, and Blaise Cronin, eds. *Conceptions of Library and Information Science: Historical, Empirical and Theoretical Perspectives: Proceedings of the International Conference Held for the Celebration of the 20th Anniversary of the Department of Information Studies, University of Tampere, Finland, 26-28 August 1991*. London: Taylor Graham, 1992.

Van House, Nancy, and Stuart Sutton. "The Panda Syndrome: An Ecology of LIS Education." *Journal of Education for Library and Information Science* 37, no. 2 (1996): 131-147.

Varoufakis, Yanis. "Marx Predicted our Present Crisis—and Points the Way Out." *The Guardian*, Friday 20 April 2018. https://www.theguardian.com/news/2018/apr/20/yanis-varoufakis-marx-crisis-communist-manifesto.

Vircillo Franklin, Carmela. "'Pro communi doctorum virorum comodo': The Vatican Library and Its Service to Scholarship." *Proceedings of the American Philosophical Society* 146, no.4 (2002): 363-384.

Vostal, Filip. *Accelerating Academia: The Changing Structure of Academic Time*. London: Palgrave-Macmillan, 2016.

Vårheim, Andreas. "Trust and the Role of the Public Library in the Integration of Refugees: The Case of a Northern Norwegian City." *Journal of Librarianship and Information Science* 46, no. 1 (2014): 62-69.

Williams, Jeffrey J. "The Rise of the Promotional Intellectual." *Chronicle of Higher Education*, August 5, 2018. https://www.chronicle.com/article/The-Rise-of-the-Promotional/244135.

Williamson, Charles C. *The Williamson Reports of 1921 and 1923: Including Training for Library Work (1921) and Training for Library Service (1923)*. Metuchen, NJ: Scarecrow Press, 1971.

Wright, Alex. *Cataloging the World: Paul Otlet and the Birth of the Information Age.* Oxford, UK: Oxford University Press, 2014.

Wright, H. Curtis. *Jesse Shera, Librarianship, and Information Science.* Sacramento, CA: Library Juice Press, 2013.

# INDEX

academic freedom, 76, 94-5
acceleration of social change, 88-90
acceleration of the pace of life, 88, 90-92
accessibility, 11, 13, 114-5
accreditation, 29, 141
Adler, Melissa, 173
agonistic pluralism, theory of, 43, 61-4, 159
Andersen, Jack, 47, 61
apprenticeship(s), 13, 15-17, 25, 71
Åström, Fredrik, 112-4, 116-7
Audunson, Ragnar, 40, 134-5
authoritarianism, 1, 43, 67

Berg, Maggie, 100-1
bibliometric indicators, 98, 102
bibliometrics, 111, 119
*Bildung*, 17-19, 55, 92, 174-5
Bologna Declaration, 25, 30, 73-8, 93, 141
Bonnici, Laurie, 141
Borup Larsen, Jeannie, 117
Brexit, 45, 148
Briet, Suzanne, 60, 130
Bruce, Harry, 129-31, 135

Buckland, Michael, 108-9, 118-21, 130-1, 174-5
Budd, John, 132-5
bureaucratic barriers, 80, 83
Burnett, Kathleen, 141
Buschman, John, 39, 66

capitalism, 19, 27, 37, 153, 170
cataloging, 31-2, 120
Chu, Heting, 141
civility, 7, 17-8. 48, 55, 58, 65, 75, 81, 171, 173, 176
classification, 8, 31-2, 89, 111, 164, 173
Clement, Claude, 10
cognitive science, 110, 161-2
cognitive viewpoint, 114, 161
cognitivism, 111
communication theory, 162-3
competence, 22, 56, 58, 83-4
competitive environment, 23, 26, 51, 77, 98, 101, 121, 137
competitiveness, 72, 84-5, 140, 142
computer science, 117, 119, 122, 126, 133, 168
complexity, 81, 86, 120, 162, 168

Conceptions of Library and Information Science (CoLIS), 105, 154, 174
conduit metaphor, 163-4
conflict, 13, 16, 31, 43-4, 46, 52, 56, 61-6, 69, 71, 80-1, 159
consensus, 39-40, 43-4, 50, 52, 63, 65, 67, 69, 71, 110
constitution, Swedish, 52-6
convergence, 113, 115-8
Cope, Jonathan, 64-5
corporate university, 37, 78, 93-4, 101
Cosette, André, 60
critical information literacy
critical thinking, 102, 154, 160, 171
cross-disciplinary, 117, 122, 160
cultural welfare, 54-5 *see also* civility
customer(s), 2, 27, 47, 75, 94, 97, 122, 150-3, 157, 170

Day, Ronald, 130, 163-4
data, 29, 89, 112, 133, 170
data curation, 3, 169
data science, 137
debate, 66, 105, 160, 170
   and conflict, 50, 52, 56
   public, 43, 45, 49, 52, 60
Dahler-Larsen, Peter, 97-8
decision-making, 50, 81, 83, 89, 130, 180
   speedy, 83, 87, 93, 103
Delisle, Leopolde, 15-16
democratic development, 24, 43, 56, 63-4, 71-2, 81, 143, 171
democratic ideals, 41, 67, 71, 80

democratic participation, 2, 4-5, 33, 39, 59, 67, 81
democracy, 19, 38, 40, 42, 46, 52, 54, 61-2, 64, 158, 171-2
   and conflict, 49, 180
   and iSchools, 153
   liberal, 13, 39, 41, 101
   and libraries, 33, 40, 44, 55, 157, 178
   social, 24, 45
deregulation, 78, 158
Dervin, Brenda, 34-5, 42-3
design, 10, 109, 119, 129, 139
Dewey, John, 173
Dewey, Melvil, 16, 20, 164
digital humanities, 115, 122, 133
digitization, 41, 89, 114, 145, 168
discomfort, 101, 133-5
divergence, 113, 117-8
diversity, 42, 50, 62, 68, 74, 138, 158, 169, 171
documentation, 60, 106, 111-2, 121-2, 131, 165-8, 176, 181
documentation movement, European, 31, 108-9, 130-1, 164
document(s), 97, 111-2, 119-20, 122, 129-33, 165-8, 173, 176, 179, 181
domain analysis, 106, 111
Downey, Annie, 173
Dumas, Catherine, 132-5

ecologies, 28, 31, 34
economic growth, 5, 26-7, 50, 63, 72-3, 76, 82, 92, 101, 137, 142-3, 170-1

economism, 73, 157
Edmundson, Mark, 94
elitism, 134, 136
Elmborg, James, 173
emancipation, 19, 61, 95-6, 150-2, 155
emancipatory resilience, 159, 178
entrepreneurial university(ies), 77-79, 81-2, 84-6, 93, 115, 136, 142, 155, 158
entrepreneur(s), 79, 85-6, 90, 150, 154
equality, 22-4, 62, 66, 171
ethics, 4, 22, 45, 58, 66, 69, 178-9 *see also* values
evaluation, 51, 176
excellence, 72-3, 136, 154

Ferraris, Maurizio, 165-6
Floridi, Luciano, 129
for-profit, 28-9, 33, 42, 78, 158
Frankfurt School, 44, 64, 87
free speech, 49, 68
freedom of expression, 52-5, 171
freedom of the press, 53
Friberg, Torbjörn, 75-7
fringe movements, 46, 63, 127, 148, 152
Frohmann, Bernd, 161, 164
funding, 24, 55
  for Library and Information Science research, 113-4, 116, 118, 126-7, 145-7
  and libraries, 5, 17, 28
  and higher education, 78, 80-1, 137, 140, 142-3, 151, 172
Furner, Jonathan, 131

general knowledge, 105, 107, 154, 174
Gesner, Konrad, 89
Giddens, Anthony, 23-4
Gilded Age, 20, 27, 150
Ginsberg, Benjamin, 93-4
Gjestrum, Liv, 134
GLAM, 116, 139
Golub, Koraljka, 135, 141
Goodman, Paul, 94-5
Google, 151, 154
Gorman, Michael, 60, 178
Graduate Library School, University of Chicago, 25, 108
Greifeneder, Elke, 130-1, 136

Habermas, Jürgen, 39-40, 44, 87
Hauptmann, Robert, 58
Heidegger, Martin, 163
hierarchical organization, 50, 83
higher education, 18, 121, 136, 155, 160, 172
  and ideals, 23, 71, 81, 177
  and industry, 28, 37, 122, 137
  restructuring of, 3-5, 26, 28, 31, 73-5, 78, 92, 101, 105, 140, 152, 154, 170
Hjørland, Birger, 106-8
Honneth, Axel, 44-5, 49, 64, 66, 87, 173
Honoré, Carl, 96
Horizon 2020, 142-53
Humboldt, Wilhelm von, 18, 75, 85, 87
human development paradigm, 171-3

Ibekwe-SanJuan, Fidelia, 110-11, 113
iConference, 122, 135, 151, 154
identity, 145, 169
   of disciplines, 138-9
   entrepreneurial, 83
   of librarianship, 159, 165, 167-8, 179, 181
   of Library and Information Science, 109, 116-7, 133, 153
ideology, 5-6, 8, 51, 83, 101, 136, 148-9, 153, 157, 159-60
iField, 69, 120, 126, 129, 132, 134, 141-2, 150, 154, 158, 161, 167
immigrants, 45, 59, 63, 68
immigration, 48-9
inclusion, 48, 69, 150-2
inertia, 29, 92, 133, 140, 150, 152, 158, 178
informatics, 133, 168
information and communication technologies (ICT), 30, 120, 143-4, 147, 163
information behavior, 31, 43, 110, 162
information industry, 26, 28-30, 33-4, 37-8, 42, 121, 123, 151-2, 154, 164, 167, 169, 181
information literacy, 6, 61, 65-6, 95, 157, 175, 180
information practices, 111-12, 162
information retrieval, 113-4, 119
information society, 1, 29, 102, 134, 165, 174
Ingwersen, Peter, 113-4

innovation, 92, 95-6, 122, 129, 142-5, 152
   and iSchools, 136
   in libraries, 28-33, 107, 121, 180
   technological, 108
institutional autonomy, 76-77
International Federation of Library Associations and Institutions (IFLA), 41, 121
iSchool brand, 132, 134, 150, 153
iSchool movement, 6, 25, 29, 69, 105, 116, 125-8, 131-2, 135-7, 142, 150, 152, 164, 166-9
iSchools Organization, 4, 118, 122-3, 125-8, 132, 135, 137, 142, 146, 151-3, 155
islamist radicalization, 147-8
internet, 29, 49, 130, 180

Järvelin, Kalervo, 113-14

Kann-Christensen, Nanna, 47, 61
Kerr, Clark, 71, 98
knowledge society, 77-8, 102
Knut (polar bear), 130-31
Koehler, Wallace, 178

Lash, Scott, 162-3
legislation, 45-6, 56-9, 61, 66, 69, 129, 180
legitimacy, 7, 11, 37-8, 45, 49, 112, 137, 146, 167,
   of Library and Information Science, 3, 38, 60, 102, 122, 151-3, 159, 161, 176-7

of librarianship, 31, 37, 40-1, 56-7, 65
of libraries, 28, 37, 57, 61, 65
of iSchools, 127, 131, 137, 155, 167
Levy, David, 166
liberal arts, 171-2, 174-5
Library Act (Sweden), 46, 53-7, 59
Library Act of Finland, 56
library education, ideals of library schools, 121, 127, 132, 140-1
Linnaeus University, 83-6, 135, 138-9
literacy skills, 84-5

Marinetti, Filippo Tommaso, 88
Mill, John Stuart, 19
morals/morality, 22, 33, 41-2, 44, 49, 62-4, 66, 84, 90, 104, 171, 177 *see also* values
Mouffe, Chantal, 61-4
Mourdoukoutas, Panos, 1-3

Nationalism, 1, 44-5, 145, 147-8
Naudé, Gabriel, 10-13, 32
new business models, 145, 151
New Public Management, 27, 48-51, 104, 176
Newman, John Henry, 177
neoliberal university, 101, 115
neoliberalism, 24-5, 39, 51, 62-3, 102, 143, 159
neutrality, 5, 95
Nicholson, Karen, 104
Nolin, Jan, 22, 112-4, 116-8
non-profit, 28, 33, 37
Nussbaum, Martha, 171-5

objectivity, 5, 95
Olson, Hope, 173
O'Neill, Maggie, 100
open access, 144, 169
Organisation for Economic Co-operation and Development (OECD), 79, 81-2

"Panda Syndrome", 29-30, 32-3, 37, 158, 169
Platina, Bartholomaeus, 8-9, 12-13
POEM, 147-9
political development, 19, 69, 81 101, 117
Pope Sixtus VI, 8-9
populist movements, 41, 63, 67, 145, 148
pragmatism, 111
private funding, 78, 80, 94, 137, 143, 151
"productivity puzzle", 74, 144, 152, 160
professionalism, 13, 66, 68
public funding, 55, 80-1, 151, 172

quantification, 68, 96, 99, 102, 119-20

rational communication, 34, 40, 42, 44, 69
recognition, theory of, 34, 42-9, 55, 59, 61-8, 159, 173
"reconquista student", 65, 76
refugees, 45, 47-8, 180
reputational autonomy, 113-4
Rivano Eckerdal, Johanna, 61, 66
Rosa, Hartmut, 87-92

scholarly communication, 42, 108, 165
scholarly publishing, 97, 168, 180
Schrettinger, Martin, 14-5, 17, 25, 32
scientific communication, 33, 64, 97, 111, 170
Seadle, Michael, 130-1, 136
Seale, Maura, 104, 157-9
Seeber, Barbara, 100-1
Seldén, Lars, 135, 141
Shannon, Claude, 162-3
Shera, Jesse Hauk, 109
"Slow Professor Manifesto", 101
Smelser, Neil, 138-40
social acceleration, 34, 86-91, 96
social development, 24, 50, 106, 143
social emancipation, 61, 95, 151, 155
social media, 1-2, 42-3, 46, 49, 97-8, 110, 166, 170
social pathologies, 45-6, 49
social science(s), 108, 114-5, 117 20, 122, 135, 144-5, 168
societal challenges, 34, 63, 71, 78, 90, 92, 95, 122, 126-7, 140, 142, 153
Socratic pedagogics, 171, 173, 176
Sorbonne Declaration, 73-4, 76
speed, 33, 38, 40, 83, 86-92, 96, 98-101, 112, 143, 163, 170
structural accretion, 137-8, 140, 150, 152
Subramaniam, Manimegalai, 141
SUITCEYES, 147, 149
Sutton, Stuart, 28-32, 38, 158

Swedish Research Council, 114, 117

technical acceleration, 88-89
technological development, 27, 44, 88, 104, 110, 112, 149, 178
theory, development of, 107-8
Toffler, Alvin, 128

uncertainty, 33, 86
undergraduate education, 74, 82, 141-2, 177
universal knowledge, 76-7, 81, 90
universalism, 34, 41, 112, 138, 161, 170
user studies, 111, 119, 162
userism, 51, 179

values, 40, 42, 46, 62, 90, 152, 170
  European, 30, 149
  and librarianship, 3-4, 28, 41, 60, 65, 68, 155, 169, 178
  societal, 81, 87, 144

Van House, Nancy, 28-30, 38, 158
vehicularity, 87, 96, 98, 139
Vostal, Filip, 72-3, 95, 99-101

Weaver, Warren, 162-3
welfare profession(s), 21-4, 180
welfare state(s), 19, 21, 24, 58, 148, 175
well-being, 92, 96, 100
Williams, Jeffrey, 98
Williamson Report(s), 17, 20-1, 25

www.ingramcontent.com/pod-product-compliance
Lightning Source LLC
Chambersburg PA
CBHW052050220426
43663CB00012B/2512